emotionally intelligent leadership

Praise for *Emotionally Intelligent Leadership for Students: A Guide for Students, Second Edition*

"This book is packed with metaphors to understand the concepts and real-life examples to bring the concepts alive. As soon as you open *Emotionally Intelligent Leadership*, the reader is taken on a personal journey of discovering and practicing EIL."

—*Cynthia Cherrey, president, International Leadership Association, and vice president, Princeton University*

"Few books exist that take the concept of leadership for college-aged students and boil it down to three discernible yet interrelated components. The authors have done a tremendous job to make this book an invaluable tool as part of an academic course on leadership or simply for one's own personal development and self-assessment."

—*Kevin W. Bailey, vice president for student affairs and program coordinator, College Student Affairs Administration Program, University of West Florida* second edition

emotionally intelligent leadership

A GUIDE FOR STUDENTS

Marcy Levy Shankman,
Scott J. Allen, and
Paige Haber-Curran

Foreword by Susan R. Komives

JB JOSSEY-BASS™
A Wiley Brand

Cover design by Wiley

Published by Jossey-Bass
A Wiley Brand
One Montgomery Street, Suite 1200, San Francisco, CA 94104-4594—www.wiley.com

Jossey-Bass books and products are available through most bookstores. To contact Jossey-Bass directly call our Customer Care Department within the U.S. at 800-956-7739, outside the U.S. at 317-572-3986, or fax 317-572-4002.

Wiley publishes in a variety of print and electronic formats and by print-on-demand. Some material included with standard print versions of this book may not be included in e-books or in print-on-demand. If this book refers to media such as a CD or DVD that is not included in the version you purchased, you may download this material at http://booksupport.wiley.com. For more information about Wiley products, visit www.wiley.com.

Library of Congress Cataloging-in-Publication Data has been applied for and is on file with the Library of Congress.

ISBN 978-1-118-82178-7 (paper); ISBN 978-1-118-93231-5 (ebk.);
ISBN 978-1-118-93232-2 (ebk.)

Printed in the United States of America

SECOND EDITION

PB Printing SKY10041691_012023

CONTENTS

FOREWORD: IT'S ALL ABOUT RELATIONSHIPS

Followers
Participants
Collaborators
Constituents
Leaders
Facilitators
Change agents

How would you combine the concepts evoked by any of these words to explain leadership? In *Exploring Leadership: For College Students Who Want to Make a Difference* (Komives, Lucas, & McMahon, 2013), we viewed leadership as "a relational and ethical process of people together attempting to accomplish positive change" (p. 95). You may think of those people as leaders and followers; however, we assert that whether in positional or nonpositional roles, people in groups engage in the process of doing leadership together.

Critical to the leadership process is the capacity of each individual to engage in authentic relationships with others and to truly understand that *leadership is all about relationships*. Thriving together by developing and maintaining healthy, effective relationships is all about emotional intelligence. Indeed, Allen and Cherrey (2000) observed, "Relationships are the connective tissue of the organizations.... Relationships built on trust and integrity, become the glue that holds us together" (p. 31). This book is designed to help you expand your personal capacity to engage effectively with others by focusing on your consciousness of self, your consciousness of others, and your consciousness of the context in which you engage in leadership together.

Expanding your relational capacity is the emotionally intelligent leadership that Marcy Levy Shankman, Scott Allen, and Paige Haber-Curran present in the second edition of this book. Consider your emotional quotient (EQ) like your intelligence quotient (IQ) and build your capacity to address intrapersonal awareness, interpersonal skills, adaptability, resilience, and general mood (Bar-On, 1997) in conjunction with how you would apply your IQ to expand your cognitive complexity. Caruso (2003) described the process we use in applying our emotional intelligence:

> We first accurately *identify* emotions. Second, we *use* these emotions to influence how we think and what we think about. Third, we attempt to *understand* the underlying causes of these emotions and determine how these emotions will change over time. Finally, we *manage* with emotions by integrating the wisdom of these feelings into our thinking, decision-making, and actions. (p. 7)

You have a marvelous opportunity in school to learn and practice emotionally intelligent leadership. As Marcy, Scott, and Paige note, you are in a remarkable "learning laboratory" where you engage with diverse peers in both classroom contexts—such as in group projects and lab experiments, service learning, campus jobs—and a broad array of co-curricular contexts ranging from intramurals or ROTC to fraternities or sororities. Further, the research from our Multi-institutional Study of Leadership (see www.leadershipstudy.net) shows that your ability to do social perspective taking, that is, seeing something from the point of view of another, is critical to your leadership capacity.

Faculty, student affairs educators, counselors, graduate students, and upper-class peers provide a ready source of mentoring or a willing ear to listen to your reflections. These supports can become companions while you intentionally stretch yourself into this leadership journey. This is a journey into yourself, into empathic understanding of others, and into sharpening your awareness of context. This book crisply helps you explore important dimensions of learning to do that well.

Learning to relate effectively to others is a developmental process. As we noted in the preface to *Exploring Leadership* (Komives et al., 2013), you would not quit learning to play tennis when serve after serve went slamming into the net or landed outside the base line—you would practice. Similarly, when you are working with others in groups you can practice the dimensions of emotionally intelligent leadership outlined in this book to help you reach a deeper, authentic understanding of others. Most of us need continual practice and skill at relating effectively with diverse others as we work together to accomplish goals and tasks.

Our research on leadership identity development (Komives, Longerbeam, Owen, Mainella, & Osteen, 2006) showed it was very common for students to think that the positional leader does leadership and that it is the role of followers to help the leader get the job done; indeed, many students would say that followers do followership. In this leader-centric philosophy of leadership, followers are dependent on the leader to set the direction and course of the group's work. As students' views of relationships develop, many come to an awareness that we are mutually dependent. The positional leader would value shared leadership and seek the active participation of group members. Group members realize they are doing leadership as active participants of the group. Each person in the group is doing leadership. One of our student participants in our research said, "I realized I can be a leader without a title." Leadership was viewed as a process among people working together in the group. This shift from hierarchical thinking to systems thinking is complex, but it is developmental.

I challenge you to practice emotionally intelligent leadership with a goal to learn the interdependence of people working together in group settings. Whether you are in a positional leadership role or serve as an active member of the group, you are doing leadership! Your authentic, ethical relationships are centrally important to the group's community and to accomplishing your shared goals. Emotionally intelligent leadership, which you will learn about as you read this book, is central to your developmental process of learning to engage with others and do leadership together. Enjoy the journey—and keep practicing!

Susan R. Komives
Coauthor of *Exploring Leadership: For College Students Who Want to Make a Difference* and coeditor of the *Handbook of Student Leadership Development and Leadership for a Better World*

References

Allen, K. E., & Cherrey, C. (2000). *Systemic leadership: Enriching the meaning of our work*. Lanham, MD: University Press of America.

Bar-On, R. (1997). *The Bar-On Emotional Quotient Inventory (EQ-i): A test of emotional intelligence*. Toronto, Canada: Multi-Health Systems.

Caruso, D. (2003). Defining the inkblot called emotional intelligence. *Issues and Recent Developments in Emotional Intelligence*, *1*(2), 1–8. www.eiconsortium.org

Komives, S. R., Longerbeam, S. D., Owen, J. E., Mainella, F., & Osteen, L. (2006). A leadership identity development model: Applications from a grounded theory. *Journal of College Student Development*, *47*(4), 401–418.

Komives, S. R., Lucas, N., & McMahon, T. R. (2013). *Exploring leadership: For college students who want to make a difference* (3rd ed.). San Francisco, CA: Jossey-Bass.

ACKNOWLEDGMENTS

We are indebted to the team at Jossey-Bass: our wonderful editor, who is truly a partner in our work, Erin Null; Alison Knowles, associate editor; and Cathy Mallon, senior production editor. Together, they have worked collaboratively with us each step of the way, pushing when we needed to be pushed and encouraging us to pause when we needed that important voice of reason. To Erin, especially, we appreciate your openness, interest in advancing the work, and stable hand that brings clarity and thoughtfulness to the work.

We appreciate all the students who took the time to share with us their experiences and thoughts about leadership. Their voice is a critical part of our work—and we couldn't have heard it without the help and support from our colleagues and friends who connected us to them. Thanks to all of you, we have created a real contribution to the field with this revised edition.

Finally, we are thankful that we have partners and families who are patient and always supportive—they keep us grounded and remind us of why we do the work we do.

Marcy dedicates this book to Rebecca and Joshua—you are my inspiration, you are our future.

Scott dedicates this book to Team Allen: Jessica, Will, Kate, and Emily.

Paige dedicates this book to the college student educators who support and challenge students as they grow and develop and to students who are committed to making the world a better place.

ABOUT THE AUTHORS

Marcy Levy Shankman, PhD, has been training and consulting in leadership development and organizational effectiveness since 1998. She is vice president for strategy and director of Leadership Cleveland at the Cleveland Leadership Center. In this role she works with leaders from a cross-section of Cleveland's community to advance their civic engagement and leadership development. Marcy is also principal of MLS Consulting, LLC, which she founded in 2001. Marcy focuses on facilitating strategic planning and visioning initiatives, organizational change and development projects, as well as leadership training and board development.

Throughout her career, Marcy has spoken professionally and written in peer-reviewed journals and professional publications on leadership, emotional intelligence, and organizational effectiveness. Her focus is on helping students of all ages, from high school students to senior level executives, to consider ways to enhance their leadership capacity.

Marcy teaches in the Non-Profit Administration Program as an instructor at John Carroll University. Marcy earned her PhD from Indiana University in higher education and student affairs, her master's in college student personnel from the University of Maryland, and her bachelor's from William and Mary in religion and anthropology. Marcy is an active volunteer and lives in Shaker Heights, Ohio, with her husband, Brett, and two children, Rebecca and Joshua.

Scott J. Allen, PhD, is associate professor of management at John Carroll University. In 2008 and 2013, Scott was voted outstanding teacher in the Boler School of Business, and he enjoys working with students of all ages. Scott earned his PhD in leadership and change from Antioch University, his master's in human resource development from Xavier University, and undergraduate degree in family social science from the University of Minnesota. His research interests include leadership development and emotionally intelligent leadership.

His research has been published in several academic journals, including the *Journal of Leadership Education*, the *Journal of Leadership Studies*, *Advances in Developing Human Resources*, and *SAM Advanced Management Journal*. Scott is the coauthor of *The Little Book of Leadership Development* and *A Charge Nurse's Guide: Navigating the Path of Leadership*.

In addition to teaching and writing, Scott conducts workshops, leads retreats, and consults across industries. Scott is a member of the Academy of Management, and the Association of Leadership Educators. He serves on the boards of the International Leadership Association, OBTS Teaching Society for Management Educators, and Beta Theta Pi Fraternity. He lives in Chagrin Falls, Ohio, with his wife, Jessica, and three children—Will, Kate, and Emily.

Paige Haber-Curran, PhD, is assistant professor and program coordinator for the student affairs in Higher Education master's program at Texas State University. In 2014 Paige was recognized with the Presidential Award for Excellence in Teaching at Texas State University. She also serves as the program coordinator for the program. Paige earned her PhD in leadership studies from the University of San Diego, her master's degree in college student personnel from the University of Maryland, and undergraduate degrees in business management and German studies from the University of Arizona.

Paige's research interests include college student leadership development, emotionally intelligent leadership, women and leadership, and gender in higher education. Her work is published in several academic journals, including the *Journal of Leadership Education*, *NASPA Journal about Women in Higher Education*, and *Educational Action Research*. She also has published a number of practitioner-focused chapters in books, including *The Handbook for Student Leadership Development*, *Emerging Issues and Practices in Peer Education*, and *Exploring Leadership Facilitation and Activity Guide*. Paige is co-editor of the forthcoming book *Advancing Women and Leadership Theory*. In 2013 she was selected as an Emerging Scholar for ACPA: College Students Educators International. Paige consults and speaks around the world on topics of leadership.

Paige is actively involved in ACPA: College Student Educators International and the International Leadership Association (ILA). She also serves as a co-lead facilitator for the LeaderShape Institute. Paige lives in Austin, Texas, with her husband, Tom, and their Portuguese Water Dogs, Ike and Murphy.

To contact the authors:

Marcy Levy Shankman: shankman@mlsconsulting.net
Scott J. Allen: sallen@jcu.edu
Paige Haber-Curran: paige.haber@gmail.com

emotionally intelligent leadership

Chapter 1 Introduction

We are thrilled that you are reading this book! We each have a genuine passion and love for the topic of leadership and have given much of our professional careers to understanding what it means to lead effectively. After all, leadership is needed in all walks of life. Whether it is at your school, in your community, or at your place of worship, people who bring about positive change are energizing. They breathe life into a cause. They bring others together in powerful ways. We hope you have worked with someone like this—someone who has inspired you to work for a vision, cause, movement, or goal. We hope you are (or will be) that person for others.

We are inspired by the potential you hold. Regardless of your interests, academic focus, aspirations, career direction, and ultimate goals, you will have many opportunities to lead others, now and for the rest of your life. This may be in a formal role in an organization, as a volunteer, in a job, or even among your friends. We hope this book will help you see effective and ineffective leadership more clearly so that you can diagnose or assess a situation with greater skill. Ultimately, every organization needs individuals who have the ability to see what is needed and intervene skillfully (Meissen, 2010). We are surrounded by leadership each and every day, and we hope this book will help you think more critically about what it means to lead effectively.

Finally, we are excited because we believe that school is the perfect place to practice leading others. The three of us each had incredible learning experiences while in high school, college, and graduate school. In many ways, those experiences have helped shape our careers. Although we each bring different values, experiences, and perspectives to the table, we believe this book can accompany and strengthen your growth and development. As you continue to explore the concept of leadership, we encourage you to get involved, become engaged, and practice leadership.

You Are in the Right Place

Just like school is a place for you to practice mathematics, physics, drama, English, and athletics, it is also an outstanding practice field or laboratory for leadership. Here are a few *real* stories of students just like you engaging in some difficult scenarios that require thoughtful practice.

After three years as an orientation leader, John was happy to accept the position of senior orientation leader. This role required him to oversee his peers in a managerial role. The transition from friend to supervisor was not easy. John received minimal respect from the orientation leaders, and they often ignored or even blatantly disobeyed his requests. He lost control of his temper and lashed out at them, not only demonstrating poor self-control but also poor friendship. How can he control his emotions better? How can he be more emotionally intelligent in his leadership?

Ty has always been an extremely sociable person, and he feeds off of relationships. His passion for working with others inspired him to lead a service immersion trip to Latin America. He adapts to the lifestyle well, but not knowing the language creates a barrier. He always viewed himself as having great interpersonal and social skills, but finds he has to adapt and quickly build relationships in a new way. Likewise, he has to influence others to do so as well. How does Ty remain flexible and inspire others given the language barrier?

Alma was promoted to a management role in her organization. She leads a team of three people, which has been a big adjustment. While working full time, she is also attending graduate school and hopes to finish her master's degree in nonprofit management within two years. On top of this, she is planning a wedding. Naturally, she is feeling pressure at work, at school, and in her relationship. She finds that she is struggling to do all three well and finds herself being short with her colleagues, classmates, and fiancé. She is constantly stressed, and her family has mentioned this to her. She knows she is in over her head, and she is struggling to ask for help and eliminate items from her plate. She wants to be known as someone who can "do it all." How does Alma successfully adjust and alter course? How will existing in a constant state of stress affect her work, school, and relationship?

Laura lands the internship of her dreams. She knows that full-time employment is offered to interns who demonstrate an exceptional work ethic, so she needs to excel. For her final presentation, she works with three other interns who attend another university. However, they have different perspectives on what it means to deliver an excellent presentation. Laura knows that this presentation is a major factor when the company considers her for employment. How can she influence the others to see her vision?

Ken is confident in his leadership abilities as he takes on the position of president of his fraternity. He was captain of sports teams in high school and involved in other organizations around campus. Unfortunately, when he stepped into this new role, it was a different story. He was met with negativity and resistance. Brothers were quick to shoot down new ideas and were slow to get involved in activities. There were some brothers who wanted to support positive change, but they made up only about 60 percent of the chapter. Ken is struggling to keep the members motivated and engaged. How does he inspire others to get behind the changes he thinks will take the chapter to the next level?

Each of these real-life examples demonstrates the many leadership opportunities and challenges that present themselves to students who want to lead. The campus environment provides a rich and plentiful array of opportunities for students to deliberately practice leadership. School and campus-based organizations, residence halls, athletic teams, classrooms, jobs, internships, and other opportunities offer a number of ways to experiment with different approaches to leadership—honing the philosophy, approaches, and styles that best suit you.

This book will help you enhance your ability to lead and think more critically about what it means to lead others. Although you may know when you are in the presence of great leadership, you may not know *why* you think that is so. One goal we have is to "pull back the curtain" and de-mystify leadership. Of course, leadership is a complex phenomenon and difficult to master, but the mystery lessens when you know how to take a closer look. In the end, we hope you will work toward becoming:

- someone who continually works at the "edge" of your abilities;
- someone who is acutely in tune with your values and acts on them;
- someone who intentionally practices leadership on and off campus;
- someone who reflects and consistently looks inward as a way to develop and grow;

- someone who is open to giving and receiving feedback;
- someone who develops relationships with ease and builds coalitions;
- someone who is inclusive;
- someone who can work through differences;
- someone who is just as skilled at following as leading; and
- someone whom others look to as a role model and guide.

Our Ten Truths about Leadership

Before introducing you to emotionally intelligent leadership (EIL), we provide some of our assumptions about the broader topic of leadership. You may disagree with some of these ideas, and that is okay. We feel these assumptions can help you succeed as you explore the practice of leadership. So if you disagree with what we've said, consider our perspective and give it a try. Then, after you've tested it for a while, you may come to a deeper understanding of your own truths. Following are the foundational ideas about leadership that influenced the development of EIL.

1. *Leadership is art and science.* Like any other domain of knowledge and practice (e.g., medicine, law, engineering), volumes of academic research have been written on what it means to be an effective leader (the science). However, this research has not resulted in a simple formula of effective leadership. It does not exist. To become a great *leader*, we must realize that there is uncertainty, there are a range of contexts, and thus, there is an art to leadership as well. In reality, great leaders know when to rely on the research (science) and when to improvise (art) to blaze a new trail.

2. *Leadership can be learned and developed.* The notion that one must be born a leader and that people cannot grow and develop leadership capacity is an archaic way of thinking. In fact, research conducted on twins found that as much as 70 percent of leadership is learned (Arvey, Rotundo, Johnson, Zhang, & McGue, 2006). This research suggests that people may be born with some genetic

predispositions that may help them more easily engage in leadership (e.g., extraversion, stamina), but the role of the environment is undeniable. From personal experience, we know that through hard work, we have improved our own capacity to lead. And we have worked with students who, through their own hard work and attention, have developed their capacity to lead others as well.

3. *Leadership is available to all.* If leadership can be learned, then it is available to all of us. We believe anyone has the ability to lead. With that being said, we know that leadership involves considerable attention, discipline, desire, and commitment. Throughout the book, we discuss the importance of *deliberate practice* when working to further develop your abilities. Deliberate practice has four primary ingredients: time, repetition, coaching/feedback, and working at the edge of your current abilities (Ericsson, Krampe, & Tesch-Römer, 1993).

4. *Leadership does not require a title or position.* Thankfully, the world is filled with people who have made a difference even though they did not have the formal authority to do so. Take a minute to see whether you can name ten people who engaged in *leadership* without having the formal title of *leader*. Many people think a rule of leadership is that you need to have a position of authority or a title to make a difference. That just simply isn't true. Although having a formal leadership role *can* have its benefits and can help you influence others, this is not a prerequisite to leading. One of the great benefits of recognizing that leadership does not require a title is knowing that you can immediately start making a difference. Join a committee, start a club, fill a need that you see, volunteer in your community, and make a difference.

5. *Leadership is more than the leader*. Early research on leadership focused primarily on men in positions of authority. The paradigm was that leaders held prominent positions (e.g., president, king, emperor) and were considered something special (they were born leaders). Today, this thinking has expanded because of what we have learned about leadership. In fact, leadership is a complex process and involves the interplay of the individual, the group, and the context. To reduce the study of leadership only to

the leader is limiting, incomplete, and misleading. In fact, each of us move in and out of the role of leader and follower—often without noticing. Much like a dance, one can step up and take on leadership and then move back into a follower's role based on the situation (Chaleff, 2011).

6. *Leadership involves bringing about positive change.* What distinguishes leadership from getting stuff done or just going through the motions is that the purpose of the leadership is to bring about positive change. Leadership involves having aspirational visions of positive change for others, an organization, a community, or a cause. We should challenge unethical practices, think of innovative ways to address opportunities or challenges, and seek to make groups, organizations, and communities better than how we found them.

7. *Leadership is an interpersonal activity.* Leadership involves engaging others in the process. Defining leadership as just a set of individual traits, skills, or behaviors is limiting. Instead, leadership is what you *do* with those leadership traits, skills, or behaviors as you engage with others. There is a leadership myth that leadership just requires charisma. This simply is not true. Charisma may initially energize others, but *leadership* engages others over the long run. It is about empowering and mobilizing others to act.

8. *No theory is the best theory.* There are dozens of leadership theories and thousands of books and articles on the topic. Each model of leadership has a new perspective, ingredient, or insight that may help *you* better develop your own personal model or understanding of what works best. Be wary of any theory that claims to "have it all." Our hope is that after you have explored leadership from several perspectives, you will have greater clarity on *your own* path and perspective. At the same time, we hope you will remain open to new ideas about leadership as you come across them. After all, learning leadership is a process.

9. *Leadership can be stressful, difficult, and even dangerous.* By nature, the activity of leading others is at minimum stressful, and at another extreme dangerous. This is where much of the work on leadership is limited. The vast majority of the literature only

describes one side of what it is like to lead, which is the positive side. We do not pretend that leadership is easy. It is difficult work. Inherent in leadership are many challenges, including an increased commitment of time; the need to manage conflict; a need to navigate the political nature of organizations; a level of ambiguity; feeling alone; risk taking; and a need or willingness to be unpopular at times. With this being said, some of the most important movements (e.g., the civil rights movement) were possible *only* because people were willing to take risks and persevere.

10. *Leadership requires inner work.* The inner work of leadership involves reflection and introspection, and it is never complete. This side of leadership development requires considerable energy, dedication, and a long-term commitment. You must commit to looking within and identifying areas in which you need to improve, develop, and grow. Through consistently and honestly reflecting, alone or with others, you can make sense of yourself and how you are interacting with others. By doing so, you will gain clarity on your own strengths, weaknesses, values, biases, and styles, which will better position you to engage with others and make a positive difference.

> Leadership can feel dangerous because you have to put yourself out there for people to see, and possibly judge, which is very scary.
>
> —*Amanda Werger, high school junior from Toronto, Ontario, involved in basketball, yearbook, drama organization, and a regional youth group*

Emotionally Intelligent Leadership

Built upon our ten truths of leadership is our model of emotionally intelligent leadership. EIL is integrative in nature (Boyer, 1990). In other words, we have combined what we feel is the best thinking on emotional intelligence and leadership into one model. For a more academic and theoretical introduction to the model see Allen, Shankman, and Miguel (2012). In the development of EIL, we have drawn upon three sources: our own experiences, the experiences of students with whom we have worked, and the literature and scholarship on emotional intelligence and leadership.

In the midst of all this, however, we want to emphasize the great value your own experiences and perspectives hold. You need to determine your own styles and approaches to leadership. We emphasize throughout the book that intentionality around your own development is central to EIL. In other words, just as with any other skill or ability, you have to *want* to develop it. Effective leadership takes commitment and awareness. Effective leadership requires changing behavior. Effective leadership takes deliberate practice.

> Being a leader in the Virginia Tech Corps of Cadets, I learned quickly that emotional intelligence determines the effectiveness of your leadership. Every day, I faced problems that affected my emotions, which in turn affected the people around me. Being aware of my actions and emotions helped me be a more effective leader.
>
> —*Christine Brenek, Virginia Polytechnic Institute and State University senior, involved in the corps of cadets*

EIL synthesizes two major bodies of research and theory: emotional intelligence (EI) and leadership. In 1990, Peter Salovey and John Mayer published a paper in which they coined the term *emotional intelligence* and define it as "the ability to monitor one's own and others' feelings and emotions to use the information to guide one's thinking and actions" (p. 189). In 1995, Daniel Goleman made EI popular in his book *Emotional Intelligence* and described it as the ability "to recognize and regulate emotions in ourselves and others" (p. 2). We believe emotional intelligence is a core function of effective leadership.

We define emotionally intelligent leadership (EIL) as promoting an intentional focus on three facets: consciousness of self, consciousness of others, and consciousness of context. Across the three EIL facets are nineteen capacities that equip individuals with the knowledge, skills, perspectives, and attitudes to achieve desired leadership outcomes.

> Emotional intelligence is a measure of the ability to be empathetic and "tuned in" to others' thoughts, feelings, and attitudes, while remaining aware of one's own thoughts, feelings, and attitudes—and, finally, considering the ways in which all of these things interact.
>
> —*John Betts, Hunter College graduate student, involved in the National Association of Social Workers*

The Three Facets of Emotionally Intelligent Leadership

Central to our definition of EIL are the three facets: consciousness of self, consciousness of others, and consciousness of context. Embedded in our truths of leadership earlier in this chapter, you read about our belief that leadership is not solely about the leader—leadership is a reciprocal relationship with others that aims to bring about positive change. Equally important, but often not recognized clearly, is that the context in which the work is being done is fundamental to success or failure. Following is how we define each of the three facets.

1. *Consciousness of Self*: Demonstrating emotionally intelligent leadership involves awareness of your abilities, emotions, and perceptions. Consciousness of self is about prioritizing the inner work of reflection and introspection and appreciating that self-awareness is a continual and ongoing process.
2. *Consciousness of Others*: Demonstrating emotionally intelligent leadership involves awareness of the abilities, emotions, and perceptions of others. Consciousness of others is about intentionally working with and influencing individuals and groups to bring about positive change.
3. *Consciousness of Context*: Demonstrating emotionally intelligent leadership involves awareness of the setting and situation. Consciousness of context is about paying attention to how environmental factors and internal group dynamics affect the process of leadership.

Although these definitions provide a clean and simple explanation, in the real world, this is not always the case. Following is a brief student case study to help explain how the three facets play out.

Rosalee is the newly elected president of the graduate student association. She is an outgoing individual and extremely achievement oriented, and she is viewed by others as being authentic, optimistic, and open to feedback from others. The executive team is another story. Rosalee did not know many members who were elected, and they have many different viewpoints, goals, and objectives. In addition, they do not necessarily like Rosalee on a personal level. To further complicate matters, the university is a male-dominated institution, and the university president is known as cold, aloof, and not especially respectful of women in leadership roles on campus. All of Rosalee's interactions with the president up until this point have been fairly disappointing.

As Rosalee begins her term, she realizes she will need to navigate the facets of consciousness of *self*, consciousness of *others*, and consciousness of *context* in a skillful manner. One could say she has some work to do in each of those realms. It is likely this situation will also require her to develop skills and relationships in places she had not foreseen.

When discussing the three facets, we use the metaphor of "signal strength" (see Figure 1.1). In the context of cellular communication and Wi-Fi networking, signal strength is something many of us are attuned to each day—after all, the strength of our signal determines our ability to connect and communicate with others to accomplish our desired tasks and goals.

Figure 1.1 Signal Strength

Here's how the metaphor works: imagine yourself as the dot. Each bar that radiates out from you represents the three facets (self, others, context—in that order). With one bar (consciousness of self), you have a certain level of success. Add one more bar, and your signal strengthens because you are in tune with yourself and others (consciousness of others). Signal strength cannot be maximized, however, until all three bars are working at full capacity. Adding the third bar means you are also conscious of the context. When you are conscious of self, others, and context, we call this working at full strength.

Now, just like the Wi-Fi network signal strength changes, so does our capacity to demonstrate EIL. Each of us moves in and out of "hot spots." In some cases we may be left with low to no signal because we are not paying attention to ourselves, others, or the context. This would result in limiting our ability to "connect." In other words, at any time we may find ourselves in a new context, and if we're not paying attention, we may find ourselves without the knowledge, skills, and abilities to succeed. The opposite is also true: when we are fully aware, maximizing our capacities, then all three bars are "lit up" and we are at full strength.

As you think about leadership, and EIL in particular, remember this simple image and metaphor. Are you working at full signal strength, or are you only focused on self? Leadership is best demonstrated when working at full signal strength. Your ability to monitor all three facets intentionally will help you to lead effectively. Anyone committed to leadership must be aware of oneself (one's knowledge, skills, and abilities); the needs, interests, and abilities of others involved; and factors from the larger environment and the group that come into play.

The Nineteen Capacities of EIL

Now that we have you thinking about the three facets of EIL, you may be wondering what those facets look like in action. EIL proposes nineteen capacities that are inherent in the three facets. The *American Heritage Dictionary* defines *capacity* as "ability to perform or produce; capability." We chose this word because we believe everyone has the capacity to engage in leadership. We believe that each of the EIL capacities is learnable and teachable. Refer to the Appendix for the complete definitions of the three facets and nineteen capacities of EIL.

When we think of effective leadership, we envision a healthy and appropriate balance of these capacities. As we have discussed, there is no fixed formula for which capacities you must demonstrate and when; suggesting so would minimize the complexities and realities of leadership. We also know that nineteen capacities can feel overwhelming. We are not claiming that you have to be excellent in all capacities; rather, we all have the nineteen capacities at our disposal to use and develop. Consider the metaphor of an orchestra. The nineteen capacities are the different instruments in the orchestra—some may come into play in some situations more than others (e.g., louder or for longer sets), but for a full concert, it is likely that each instrument needs to be present at some level. So, while in a certain situation, we may only need to intentionally use a core set of seven EIL capacities, we know there are nineteen to choose from.

As stated previously, effective leadership is about having an appropriate balance among the capacities. It is not effective or advisable to demonstrate any one of these capacities to excess. Any strength taken to an extreme can become a limitation. At the same time, underusing any capacity can also have negative repercussions. For instance, with too much emphasis on *building teams*, a group can become bogged down, even paralyzed, thus keeping the team from progressing and moving forward.

Consciousness of Self

Emotional self-perception: Identifying emotions and their influence on behavior
Emotional self-control: Consciously moderating emotions
Authenticity: Being transparent and trustworthy
Healthy self-esteem: Having a balanced sense of self
Flexibility: Being open and adaptive to change
Optimism: Having a positive outlook
Initiative: Taking action
Achievement: Striving for excellence

Consciousness of Others

Displaying empathy: Being emotionally in tune with others
Inspiring others: Energizing individuals and groups
Coaching others: Enhancing the skills and abilities of others
Capitalizing on difference: Benefiting from multiple perspectives
Developing relationships: Building a network of trusting relationships
Building teams: Working with others to accomplish a shared purpose
Demonstrating citizenship: Fulfilling responsibilities to the group
Managing conflict: Identifying and resolving conflict
Facilitating change: Working toward new directions

Consciousness of Context

Analyzing the group: Interpreting group dynamics
Assessing the environment: Interpreting external forces and trends

At the other extreme, if *building teams* is ignored, people can feel alienated. This often results in one person from the group doing all the work.

The bottom line is to make sure that the balance is dynamic—it is continually shifting based on the context. In other words, the appropriate demonstration or use of a capacity in one situation may be inadequate in another situation, based on the individual, the group, and the context. That's one of the reasons why EIL is comprised of both the facets (paying attention to what is happening and who is involved) and the capacities (doing what is needed).

What Lies Ahead: How to Use This Book

Over the years we have been told that the first edition of this book has been used in a number of ways: resident advisor training, executive board training in student organizations, academic courses, co-curricular leadership programs, high schools, student employment settings, graduate classes, academic conferences, summer camps, workshops, and the list goes on. Although each example may not apply to your current setting (high school, college, graduate school), we encourage you to see how each of these concepts applies in your life. Although we have chosen school as the focus, we know that these concepts apply to health care, education, business, engineering, and so on. If you find an interesting, unique use, please share your experience. We want to hear your feedback.

One reason for the widespread use of this book is that it is intended to be a fast read. The chapters are short and contain key concepts related to the facets or capacities that we think are most important to consider. We have also included student quotes throughout. Of course, full textbooks could be written (and are written) on many of these topics. Recognize that our intention is to help you sort through that information and provide what we think will be most useful to your development.

The book is interactive and not academic in tone, yet it is rooted in sound academic thought. We would like you to dig deeper into our sources if you have an interest. You can see Allen et al. (2012) for a more academic paper on EIL. At points, you may think that we are simply sharing what amounts to common sense—you may say, "I know that!" Good. The next question to ponder is "Do I *do* that? . . . With excellence?" In others words, *common sense does not equal common practice*. Each of us can improve, grow, and develop. This book is meant to introduce you to EIL and encourage you to think about what it means to you. If you want to learn how to demonstrate the capacities and facets of EIL, enhance your leadership capacity, or teach others about EIL, then you'll appreciate our other publications on EIL—the second editions of *Emotionally Intelligent Leadership for Students: Student Workbook*, *Emotionally Intelligent Leadership for Students: Inventory*, and *Emotionally Intelligent Leadership for Students: Facilitation and Activity Guide*.

Another purpose of this book is to get you thinking about how strengths in one context may become limitations in another. At the end of each chapter, specific questions are offered to deepen your thinking about this and other related issues and opportunities. We include quotes from a variety of students in each chapter to help you understand the concepts through their eyes. We hope these quotes and the reflection questions help you connect with the material more meaningfully. Our other resources will help you reflect on your behaviors and how these concepts and capacities apply to your life.

Finally, we suggest talking with close friends, colleagues, or mentors about what you read. If you have these conversations, we believe you will receive feedback that will help you identify existing areas of strength and opportunities for growth. We also encourage you to discuss the content with individuals whom you believe to have different or even critical perspectives. After all, a family member knows you in a different way than your volleyball coach does. Each has valuable information to contribute toward your development and growth. We wish you an enjoyable and insightful ride as you engage with this material and consider ways to apply EIL in your life.

References

Allen, S. J., Shankman, M. L., & Miguel, R. (2012). Emotionally intelligent leadership: An integrative, process-oriented theory of student leadership. *Journal of Leadership Education, 11*(1), 177–203.

Arvey, R. D., Rotundo, M., Johnson, W., Zhang, Z., & McGue, M. (2006). The determinants of leadership role occupancy: Genetic and personality factors. *Leadership Quarterly, 17*, 1–20.

Boyer, E. (1990). *Scholarship reconsidered: Priorities of the professoriate.* (Eric-Document Reproduction Service No. ED326149).

Chaleff, I. (2011, May 30). *Leadership and followership: What tango teaches us about these roles in life.* [Video file]. http://www.youtube.com/watch?v=Cswrnc1dggg

Ericsson, K. A., Krampe, R. Th., & Tesch-Römer, C. (1993). The role of deliberate practice in the acquisition of expert performance. *Psychological Review, 100*(3), 363–406.

Goleman, D. (1995). *Emotional intelligence.* New York, NY: Bantam Books.

Goleman, D. (2000). Leadership that gets results. *Harvard Business Review*, March-April, 78–90.

Meissen, G. (2010). Leadership lexicon. *Journal of Kansas Civic Leadership Development, 2*(1), 78–81.

Salovey, P., & Mayer, J. D. (1990). Emotional intelligence. *Imagination, Cognition, and Personality, 9*(3), 185–211.

Part One: Consciousness of Self

Chapter 2 Consciousness of Self

Demonstrating emotionally intelligent leadership involves awareness of your abilities, emotions, and perceptions. Consciousness of self is about prioritizing the inner work of reflection and introspection and appreciating that self-awareness is a continual and ongoing process.

The Intrapersonal Dimension of Leadership

If you step back and think about your life until this point, you will likely agree that it is a fascinating story. Many of you reading this book have experienced great achievement, overcome adversity, and worked with others to make a difference. In fact, if you think of yourself even three years ago, it is likely you have grown and developed in many ways. We see leadership development in a similar light. Leadership is not a basic skill that can be mastered in one or two years. Developing leadership is a lifelong journey filled with successes, hardships, and deliberate practice. Leadership can be learned, and to do so takes a great deal of intentional thought and practice.

Emotionally intelligent leadership (EIL) requires a focus on three primary facets: self, others, and context. Part I of this book focuses on the inner dimension of EIL—we call this *consciousness of self*. Demonstrating EIL means being aware of yourself in a number of ways, especially being deeply in tune with your emotions, values, strengths, limitations, and worldview. By doing so, you focus your energy on a crucial element of effective leadership: self-awareness (Avolio & Gardner, 2005; Conger, 1992). The path toward self-awareness is a process of growth and development and requires an ongoing and long-term commitment (Avolio & Gibbons, 1989).

A key aspect of self-awareness is understanding your abilities. Some people tend to underestimate their abilities, which poses challenges. Arguably, what poses greater challenge is when people *overestimate* their abilities (Kruger & Dunning, 1999). Two scholars coined this the Dunning-Kruger effect, whereby "people are incompetent in the strategies they adopt to achieve success and satisfaction, they suffer a dual burden: Not only do they reach erroneous conclusions and make unfortunate choices, but their incompetence robs them of the ability to realize it" (p. 1121). When we demonstrate consciousness of self we are seeking to combat the Dunning-Kruger effect. Next, we share three fundamental steps that will help you along this path: prioritizing self-awareness, seeking feedback, and reflecting.

Making Self-Awareness a Priority

> I believe the way to develop great self-awareness as a leader and individual all comes down to stepping out of one's comfort zone. If you are able to step out of your comfort zone, try new things, and take risks, it helps you raise awareness about skills and hidden knowledge.
> —*Sean Ryan, University of Iowa recent graduate, involved in associated residence halls and as an orientation leader*

So where do you begin? First, you need to decide that self-awareness is a priority. Leadership scholars Day, Harrison, and Halpin (2009) suggest "self-awareness is critical for leader development and success. Research has empirically linked self-awareness and managerial performance across a variety of organizational contexts" (p. 198). To make this commitment, you must demonstrate the necessary motivation to look within and have a desire to engage in continual reflection. This takes deliberate practice. If you are not working to better understand your motives, values, and inner workings, who will? It is not important that this introspection results in concrete answers—it is the *process* of introspection that is important (Avolio, 2004). To begin this process we suggest developing reflection as a habit and seeking feedback to support you in this process.

Seeking Feedback

Surrounding yourself with peers and mentors who are willing to give you unfiltered and honest feedback will make a difference in your ability to be self-aware. "A leader's lack of self-awareness may reveal a lack of listening, a lack of response to followers' demands, and a lack of attention to criticism and failures—a misdiagnosis of the leader's strengths and weaknesses" (Bass, 2008, p. 185). We all have blind spots, and others are likely to identify ways we can improve. One of the best ways to increase consciousness of self is to seek feedback from people who know you well. Although it may be difficult to ask, feedback contributes significantly to enhancing your self-understanding.

Perhaps the most challenging aspects of asking for feedback are the initial request for feedback and the ability to hear it. Most people, when asked whether they like getting feedback, say "No." This is often true for positive as well as negative feedback. For some, hearing a compliment is as difficult as hearing a criticism. One of Paige's favorite phrases when she provides feedback to her students or when she encourages students to provide feedback to each other is "Feedback = Love." In fact, she writes this on the whiteboard in class and refers to it often. We honestly believe that giving and receiving feedback is an act of love. It demonstrates that someone cares enough about you to help you improve.

Each of us has people we can look to for feedback. We know they have our best interests at heart. Many of us have mentors who have shaped who we are today. We have parents, friends, neighbors, classmates, teachers, supervisors, coworkers,

> Peer-to-peer and advisor reviews are excellent ways to learn about yourself when it comes to leadership.
> —*Jeff Martin, University of Arkansas sophomore, involved in associated student government and as a student television reporter, admissions-orientation mentor, student ambassador, and resident advisor*

and coaches who have given us feedback over the years. Remember, people who are offering feedback are trying to be helpful. Learning how to be gracious about what is said is a challenge. One way to show appreciation, regardless of the feedback, is to show gratitude and thank them for investing in you enough to provide the feedback.

One last important point: You *always* have a choice in what you accept to be true. You may agree immediately, you may reject the feedback as being off base, or you may find the feedback helpful down the road. Regardless, appreciate what is offered, contemplate what is said, sort through how accurate it might be, then decide whether to accept it. Contemplating and accepting this feedback is an opportunity to heighten your self-awareness, which in turn will help you become more effective as a leader. This takes time, which is why reflection is important.

> Self-awareness can be developed simply by acknowledging that you have a place in the world and that every action has a reaction.
> —*Leanna Lakeram, Florida State University junior, involved in the social justice living learning community*

Make Reflection a Habit

In addition to seeking feedback, we also have many opportunities to learn more about ourselves through reflection. These opportunities are occasions for enhancing our self-understanding; however, we often miss these moments. We are too busy or we dwell on situations rather than seek to learn from them. We look ahead rather than reflect on what is happening in the present or what happened in the past. We can get so caught up in "doing" that we do not realize that thinking and feeling are just as important.

Reflection can be an interactive process. Reflection, in all forms, can become a habit and is a pivotal tool for continual and ongoing development. As Avolio (1999) suggests, "We must be very conscious of the past, but not so tightly bound to it that we can't move in new directions with equally new challenges. We must know where we want to go, which may take time and some data collection" (p. 28).

When you capitalize on these opportunities for reflection, you replenish your own resources. By reflecting on what has happened, you take time to think through your actions, think about how your actions may have affected others, see links or connections that you may have not realized, or identify ways in which you could have behaved differently. For leaders to be effective, they must know themselves. As author and founder of the American Leadership Forum, Joe Jaworski says, "Before you can lead others, before you can help others, you have to discover yourself" (Webber, 1996).

A Focus on Self

Consciousness of self is an essential component of leadership; further, it serves as a necessary foundation to enact the eight capacities of this facet:

1. Emotional self-perception
2. Emotional self-control
3. Authenticity
4. Healthy self-esteem
5. Flexibility
6. Optimism
7. Initiative
8. Achievement

Part One introduces you to these eight capacities, which encompass the skills, abilities, and other characteristics that are essential for self-awareness and self-development. Two of the capacities (emotional self-perception and emotional self-control) are closely linked with emotional intelligence, while the other six capacities (authenticity, healthy self-esteem, flexibility, optimism, initiative, and achievement) blend emotional intelligence with leadership.

We suggest you can learn and enhance each of these capacities. You can continually monitor and reflect on how you are doing in each capacity and adjust or adapt accordingly. For instance, if you have your heart set on a certain course of action and others feel differently, how do you display the capacity of flexibility? Are you rigid and unyielding, or do you easily create space for the thoughts and ideas of others? Likewise, if you are working with difficult people, do they quickly trigger your hot buttons, causing you to become angry (emotional self-perception and emotional self-control)? Or can you keep your emotions in check and respond appropriately based on the needs of the situation (emotional self-control)?

As you read, think about recent experiences with family, friends, and others. As you do so, you will begin the process of reflecting with an increased level of intentionality. When you do this, you uncover greater understanding of the successes, failures, and struggles you have encountered along the way. Likewise, talk with others and learn more about their perspectives. All of this will help you further develop consciousness of self.

Student Voices

It is important to recognize that no one person is perfect. By striving to learn from one's mistakes, a person can begin to develop greater self-awareness. If people begin to take a moment out of their day to learn just one new fact or piece of information, then they will become more well rounded and obtain consciousness of self.

—*Colin Christopher McGauley, Loyola University Chicago sophomore, involved in leadership for social change learning community, tennis, and as a student ambassador and youth basketball coach*

Take time for yourself: live, laugh, love, and, eat ice cream.

—*Samantha Lyons, University of Michigan sophomore, involved in a community service fraternity, running club, and the club sports council*

A lot has to do with personality, but experience plays a big part. You have to ask yourself how far you're willing to test your limits and step out of your comfort zone to better understand yourself.

—*Jasmine Ramon, Alfred University sophomore, involved in women's leadership academy, women's soccer, and a diversity organization*

By pushing your limits and trying new things, you discover what you can truly accomplish and what sort of impact you can make. I develop my self-awareness by extending myself beyond my comfort zone.

—*Brooke Pankau, Rollins College senior, involved in student government association, student life committee, and as a peer mentor*

References

Avolio, B. J. (1999). *Full range leadership: Building the vital forces in organizations.* Thousand Oaks, CA: Sage.

Avolio, B. J. (2004). Examining the full range model of leadership: Looking back to transform forward. In D. Day & S. Zaccarro (Eds.), *Leadership development for transforming organizations: Grow leaders for tomorrow* (pp. 71–98). Mahwah, NJ: Erlbaum.

Avolio, B. J., & Gardner, W. L. (2005). Authentic leadership development: Getting to the root of positive forms of leadership. *Leadership Quarterly, 16*, 315–338.

Avolio, B., & Gibbons, T. (1989). Developing transformational leaders: A life span approach. In J. Conger & R. Kanungò (Eds.), *Charismatic leadership: The elusive factor in organizational effectiveness* (pp. 276–308). San Francisco, CA: Jossey-Bass.

Bass, B. (2008). *The Bass handbook of leadership: Theory, research and managerial applications* (4th ed.). New York, NY: Free Press.

Conger, J. (1992). *Learning to lead: The art of transforming managers into leaders.* San Francisco, CA: Jossey-Bass.

Day, D. V., Harrison, M. M., & Halpin, S. M. (2009). *An integrative approach to leader development: Connecting adult development, identity, and expertise.* New York, NY: Routledge.

Kruger, J., & Dunning, D. (1999). Unskilled and unaware of it: How difficulties in recognizing one's own incompetence lead to inflated self-assessments. *Journal of Personality and Social Psychology, 77*(6), 1121–1134.

Webber, A. M. (1996, June/July). *Destiny and the job of the leader.* www.fastcompany.com

Reflection Questions

- What would your peers say about your leadership abilities? How about a former coach or mentor?

- How do you handle hearing feedback from others?

- How do you approach new situations, new ideas, and new people? When do you have great energy? Great caution?

- When was the last time you had a major insight into your personality? What did this help you discover about yourself?

Chapter 3 Emotional Self-Perception

Identifying emotions and their influence on behavior. **Emotional self-perception is about describing, naming, and understanding your emotions. Emotionally intelligent leaders are aware of how situations influence emotions and how emotions affect interactions with others.**

Emotional self-perception is one of the four emotionally intelligent leadership (EIL) capacities most closely linked to emotional intelligence. Emotional self-perception is a difficult capacity to master because being acutely aware of emotions and how they influence your interactions with others is a continual and ongoing challenge. The energy and attention that emotional self-perception requires can be exhausting. Yet, emotionally intelligent leaders recognize how situations influence their emotions (Petrides, Sangareau, Furnham, & Frederickson, 2006; Mayer & Salovey, 1997). In essence, this requires that you be in tune with your emotions—all the time. What follows is a snapshot of what happens when emotional self-perception is lacking and what it means to be in tune with yourself.

Importance of Emotional Self-Perception

Demonstrating emotional self-perception means knowing yourself well enough to identify your emotional responses as well as being conscious of how you react emotionally to situations, people, and social dynamics. As you become aware of your natural default responses, you develop a higher level of consciousness and action. Aligning this capacity with leadership, you can see the importance of this skill. Consider the following case:

Jose is the leader of the university programming board, and the officers are preparing for a large event on campus. Jose is consistently having trouble getting others to follow through with tasks and assignments. As a result, he has become increasingly frustrated. Rather than managing the conflict appropriately or asking why others are not completing their jobs, he completes a great majority of tasks on his own. This, in turn, increases his frustration even more. His increased frustration has negatively affected members of the group—even those who are fulfilling their responsibilities. This has led those members to also become frustrated. Others on the team begin talking behind Jose's back and feel left out. By the time the event is over, there is a large gap between Jose and the officers—Jose blames the officers, and they blame him for taking over. The issue is never resolved, and many members decrease their level of involvement with the board. Jose leaves his role feeling frustrated, burnt out, and angry at the others. Further, the friendships he had with members in the group prior to taking on his role in the organization have fizzled.

This scenario is not all that uncommon. It happens in student organizations at all levels (high school, college, and graduate school) and group projects for class all too frequently. In our experience, students who take on leadership roles are generally achievement oriented and expect a lot from themselves *and* others—sometimes too much. So how does this situation relate to emotional self-perception? In large part, Jose lacked the awareness that his approach was not working and, as such, he and others became more and more frustrated. His frustrations got the best of him, and he became ineffective. His lack of emotional self-perception was a barrier for him. For whatever reason, his message or style was not connecting with others. He ignored his feelings, turned away from the real issues, and instead just dealt with the tasks on his own, which left him feeling burnt out and angry. In this scenario, Jose was, in fact, a big part of the dysfunction of the group.

With Jose's situation, and many others like this, anger, resentment, and even apathy set in. People often make comments that increase the gap between themselves and group members. In the preceding scenario, if Jose had been acutely aware of his feelings and how they affected his ability to lead, he could have confronted the issue in a constructive manner at the beginning and, perhaps, avoided the whole problem. Instead, lacking emotional self-perception led Jose down a different, more difficult path.

Jose could have learned a lot through reflection. If he had identified for himself first what he was feeling, he could have then engaged in open dialogue with his officers to better understand their apathy and lack of motivation. Of course, the situation was not totally Jose's fault, but if his goal was to *lead* the organization through a successful event, letting his aggravation get the best of him did not help the situation. After all, who wants to be led by an individual who is inconsistent, lacks self-awareness, and is unaware of how his emotions and actions affect those around him?

> Being aware of your emotions allows you to see that every person represents a different piece of a puzzle. A good leader sees every piece as unique yet sees all pieces as part of one big puzzle.
> —*Monica Hernandez, University of Texas School of Public Health graduate student, involved in student society for global health*

No one wants to be *that* person—especially not you. Emotionally intelligent leaders must work consistently to remain connected with their feelings and actively explore the source of their emotions. By doing so, they can work to regulate their emotions (see chapter 4 on emotional self-control) and intentionally choose an appropriate response to yield desired results.

Being in Tune

Paul Ekman is a psychologist and a leader in the study of emotions. Based on his research, Ekman (1999) concluded that human beings experience six basic emotions: anger, surprise, happiness, fear, sadness, and disgust. Think for a moment about your brother, sister, or another family member who has the ability to get under your skin. This person's comments, actions, and behaviors take your level of anger from 0 to 10 in mere seconds. We assume (if you are like us) that, at times, you may go directly to 10 *and then react*. How you react may be through yelling, crying, shutting down, putting the other person down, or any number of other immediate responses. Your reactions may be emotional (feeling angry), behavioral (yelling), or both.

> Letting your emotions control you can lead to quick, rash decisions that don't help you in the end. If you are aware of these emotions, you can put yourself above them and think critically in order to determine the best approach to a situation.
>
> —*Daniel Handel, University of Wisconsin Madison senior, involved in Greek life, a student leadership program, and as a student supervisor*

Emotional self-perception means you have the ability to be acutely aware of how you are feeling in real time. In other words, you are aware that anger levels are rising *as they are rising*. This is also known as reflection in action (Torbert, 2004). With this being said, Ashkanasy (2003) suggests that at times some emotions (e.g., anger or fear) may be only "partially under our control" (p. 14). This makes emotional self-perception very difficult and complex, but being aware of our emotions is crucial. The more we focus on being in tune with our emotions, the easier it becomes, and the better we can then become at controlling our emotions and reactions (see chapter 4 on emotional self-control).

Emotional Insight

> When I find myself in emotionally challenging situations, I take a step back and ask, "How would someone with no personal ties to this situation react?" It helps me define which of my emotions are logical emotions.
>
> —*Colin Neidert, John Carroll University graduate student, works in the consumer packaged food industry*

It is important to practice observing your feelings as you work to develop emotional self-perception. Pay close attention to your emotional state in your activities, on your athletic team, with your friends, and in your classrooms. Each and every day actively reflect on the following questions: How do I react to other people given the different situations I find myself in? Do I consciously understand how my emotions affect my behavior? Do I consciously understand how my emotions influence others? Developing this habit of assessing how you're doing on a daily basis will increase your emotional self-perception.

Another way to gain emotional insight is to look at your most recent posts on your most-used social media site. What are you telling others by the tone and message in your own posts? Pay close attention to how you use emotion to energize, elevate, and engage others. You may want to pay even closer attention to how you may struggle to remain aware of your emotions when you are not feeling upbeat. How does this affect you and others?

It is also important to observe your reaction to the emotional state of *others*. Become a student of emotions and you will experience a difference in your daily life as well as your practice of leadership. While emotional self-perception is about *your* ability to monitor emotions, it is important to become skilled in observing how others influence your emotional state as well.

Student Voices

When individuals on my hall were being disrespectful last semester, I definitely gained the respect of the rest of the community when I didn't react immediately, as I would've liked; after a few days, we all talked about the issue as a group and came up with solutions. While it may not be as immediately satisfying as sinking to someone's level, taking that step back from your emotions can be instrumental in gaining respect and cooperation in the long term from the group as a whole. And it likely stopped the issue more effectively than the inevitable escalation, confrontation, and so on.

—*Maring Eberlein, Goucher College junior, involved in campus programming board, the equestrian team, and as a tour guide*

Being aware of your emotions can help you foster healthy and constructive relationships, and help you make the best decisions for your organization and its members.

—*Jason Castillo Sanchez, The Catholic University of America senior, involved in a Filipino cultural organization, the Society of Hispanic Professional Engineers, and the chemistry club*

A leader who understands his or her emotions will set an example for the team to follow. Understanding your emotions will also allow you to control your emotions and remain a positive example to your team.

—*Kaitlyn Fitzgerald, Arizona State University junior, founder of women's global awareness organization and involved in community outreach*

When you know yourself and how you think and act, you can use that to look at yourself and how you affect other people. When you can see your effect on a group and their reactions, you can change your way of thought and actions to better lead the group.

—*Victoria Troche, Central Connecticut State University junior, involved in student programming board*

References

Ashkanasy, N. M. (2003). Emotions in organizations: A multilevel perspective. In F. Dansereau and F. J. Yammarino (Eds.), *Research in multi-level issues, vol. 2: Multi-level issues in organizational behavior and strategy* (pp. 9–54). Oxford, UK: Elsevier Science.

Ekman, P. (1999). Basic emotions. In T. Dalgleish & T. Power (Eds.), *The handbook of cognition and emotion* (pp. 45–60). Sussex, UK: Wiley.

Mayer, J. D., & Salovey, P. (1997). What is emotional intelligence? In P. Salovey & D. Sluyter (Eds.), *Emotional development and emotional intelligence: Educational implications* (pp. 3–34). New York, NY: Basic Books.

Petrides, K. V., Sangareau, Y., Furnham, A., & Frederickson, N. (2006). Trait emotional intelligence and children's peer relations at school. *Social Development, 15*(3), 537–547.

Torbert, B. (2004). *Action inquiry: The secret of timely and transforming leadership.* San Francisco, CA: Berrett-Koehler.

Reflection Questions

- In the scenario described at the beginning of the chapter, what would you suggest Jose could have done differently to better lead his organization?

- Brainstorm twelve emotions you have felt in the past week. Which were most powerful? When did you experience them? What patterns do you notice, if any?

- When have you used your emotions to positively influence others? When have your emotions negatively affected others?

- Who energizes you as a leader? As a follower? What happens when you are around people whom you find energizing? How do you feel?

Chapter 4 Emotional Self-Control

Consciously moderating emotions. **Emotional self-control means intentionally managing your emotions and understanding how and when to demonstrate them appropriately. Emotionally intelligent leaders take responsibility for regulating their emotions and are not victims of them.**

One direct manifestation of emotional self-perception is emotional self-control. Effectively, this means we take responsibility for regulating our emotions and recognize that we do not have to be victims *of* them. Anyone who has led others knows the stress inherent in doing so. Not only are you leading a group from point A to point B, you are often navigating the stress inherent in moving toward an unknown. Maintaining a level head and remaining calm can be difficult. Like an Olympic gymnast or a world-class musician, one task of leadership is to complete a variety of challenges with a sense of grace and composure. This is just one example of emotional self-control. Each of us has had a classmate, coach, parent, teacher, coworker, or supervisor who struggled with this capacity.

> Leaders are looked upon as the prime example for how to react to tough situations. Thus, a leader needs to manage his or her emotions in the face of hardship.
>
> —*Alice Chang, Claremont McKenna College junior, involved in nonprofit consulting and as an Asian Pacific American mentor*

Another way of looking at emotional self-control is to consider self-regulating. Leadership scholar Gary Yukl (2010) discusses self-regulation as "the ability to channel emotions into behavior that is appropriate for the situation, rather than responding with impulsive behavior (e.g., lashing out at someone who made you angry, or withdrawing into a state of depression after experiencing disappointment)" (p. 213). Closely linked to emotional intelligence, we could write volumes on emotional self-control. However, we will focus on three areas for practice: navigating stress, managing hot buttons, and regulating responses.

Navigating Stress

M. Scott Peck, a famous psychologist, wrote the book *The Road Less Traveled.* He begins with a very simple statement: "Life is difficult" (Peck, 2003, p. 15). We have altered his thoughts by replacing one word: "*Leadership* is difficult." Inherent in any leadership challenge is stress. Stress may come from the environment, interpersonal conflict, the nature or amount of work, or simply the uncertainty of what lies ahead. As a result, those involved can find themselves in a state of disequilibrium, which can be productive and beneficial, but also adds stress. The ability to diagnose the kind of stress you are experiencing can help you manage your emotions more effectively. Four sources of stress are common in the context of leadership: situational, encounter, anticipatory, and time (Whetten & Cameron, 2010).

1. *Situational stressors*: These sources of stress are often brought on by unfavorable working conditions and rapid change. Leaders and followers work long hours under crisis, and it is not uncommon that dynamics change quickly. In others words, leaders and followers have little control over their situation. Each of us knows a number of student leaders working to manage this source of stress. Perhaps they are overextended, there is a family emergency, or a professor has given a last-minute assignment.

2. *Encounter stressors*: These stressors stem from personal disagreements on issues. Encounter stressors usually occur between individuals or differing factions in the group (e.g., one group

in the organization wants to haze members, while another does not). It is likely you have experienced this type of stress on more than one occasion. For instance, resident advisors (RAs) navigate these kinds of stressors on a daily basis when seeking to serve the residents, larger department, and school—all of whom may have conflicting desires and needs.

3. *Anticipatory stressors*: These stressors occur when individuals are experiencing unpleasant expectations or fear. For example, a group may need to address the "elephant in the room" (e.g., an issue that everyone knows about but no one wants to discuss or admit) or confront a difficult situation. In addition, an individual may experience anticipatory stress ahead of an exam, presentation, or interview.

4. *Time stressors*: These stressors often occur due to work overload. Many student organizations pack a lot of activity into a short span of time (e.g., homecoming). This overload undoubtedly causes stress. A hallmark of time stressors is the feeling that you do not have control over your schedule. Likewise, there is a feeling of having too much to do in too little time. Although some of this may be out of our control (e.g., class assignments), a good number of time stressors are under our control. Learning to say "No" or prioritizing are skills that can be practiced and developed in a collegiate setting.

> I try to remember that I am the example. What I do affects others around me. When I think of the responsibility I hold, it helps me manage my emotions.
>
> —*Sena Belgard, University of Utah senior, involved in residence life, associated students, and as an honors college intern*

Your awareness of these stressors is an important first step in managing your emotions. By naming the stressors, you can more objectively examine and navigate the challenges they cause for you as a formal or informal leader and how they tend to impact your emotions. You can also help others make sense of their own stressors. By doing so, you are managing the emotions of the group as well, which is a key capacity of emotionally intelligent leadership (see chapter 22 on analyzing the group).

Managing Your Hot Buttons

In large measure, moderating your emotions requires a great deal of self-awareness: having an acute awareness of the stressors that trigger you to react in certain ways. A "hot button" is a stimulus that triggers an instinctive reaction, such as butterflies in your stomach or fierce anger. This reaction is part of your biological make-up and is influenced by your past experiences. As human beings we are programmed to have a flight-or-fight reaction to certain stressors.

> In order to effectively manage my emotions, I have learned to gather many perspectives about an occurrence or event before forming or sharing my opinion. By asking questions, I usually learn more about certain scenarios, and I allow myself time for emotions to subside.
>
> —*Daniel DeHollander, University of Arizona graduate student, involved in the Disney College Program alumni association and as a Greek Life graduate intern and student affairs outreach graduate assistant*

What topics or issues cause your heart to race? Are there certain subjects about which you feel intense passion? Are there people who elicit a strong emotional response in you that is difficult to manage or control? Knowing your hot buttons and anticipating when they might be pushed are important steps toward mastering the capacity of emotional self-control. Identifying these triggers enables you to prevent instinctive reactions as your default responses. You cannot control the trigger and may not be able to control the emotional impulse, but you can regulate your thoughts, decisions, and behaviors that stem from these triggers and impulses. For example, emotional self-control means that you know yourself well enough to prevent yourself from exploding with rage, and instead, you rationally navigate the situation that triggers you. This is a crucial skill for all of us. When you manage your emotions, you are demonstrating a core capacity of emotionally intelligent leadership.

Pay close attention to your hot buttons. Notice who triggers your hot buttons and reflect on why this happens. Pay attention to certain situations and people that lead you to have emotional impulses. By doing so, you can become more regulated and controlled in your reactions to stressors. Explore this topic further by taking an online *Hot Buttons Test* (Center for Conflict Dynamics, 2013; see References for link).

Regulating Your Response

Based on your knowledge of stress and the hot buttons that trigger you to react inappropriately, you develop greater control of your responses. After a great deal of practice, you can instinctively move to a place of perspective taking (perhaps displaying empathy) versus reacting in a destructive or disruptive manner (e.g., yelling uncontrollably at someone). McCauley and Van Velsor (2003) suggest, "The capacity for self management enables leaders to develop positive and trusting relationships and to take initiative—important aspects of roles that people work together in productive and meaningful ways" (p. 12). The ultimate objective is working with people in productive and meaningful ways—even if and when *they* are not modeling this behavior. This involves a great deal of intentionality, which is a core aspect of emotionally intelligent leadership.

We emphasize that emotional self-control is not about ignoring or disregarding our emotions. Emotions help us lead because they help us recognize when we might be going off track, when there is an ethical dilemma, or when something or someone requires additional attention. Emotional self-control is about intentionally managing our emotions (e.g., staying calm under stress), maintaining a level head, and understanding how and when to demonstrate emotions appropriately.

> I think if you live long enough, you realize that so much of what happens in your life is out of your control, but how you respond to it is in your control.
> —*Hillary Rodham Clinton, former U.S. Secretary of State*

This self-management relates to not only the emotions mentioned already, like anger or frustration, but also enthusiasm and joy. Emotional self-control helps us realize that we have to consider how to demonstrate our emotions effectively and appropriately. It is possible, for instance, to be too enthusiastic. Emotional self-control, and EIL for that matter, recognizes that emotions are an important part of life. Emotions affect our thoughts, decisions, and behaviors. At the heart of leadership is emotion. Emotionally intelligent leaders learn how to use their emotions with purpose.

Student Voices

Managing your emotions is not as easy as turning a switch and saying that they are "off." It takes discipline to manage the emotions that one has, especially when you want to attack back. I think the best strategy is to have someone help you. Leaders should always have a person who can be there for them—that can straighten them out. This person can be the one that can help you in certain situations while you learn to become more disciplined.

—*Guadalupe Arce Jimenez, North Carolina State University senior, involved in a Latino/a cultural organization and the diversity commission for student government*

Managing emotions is crucial for a student leader. You need to know how to respond to pressure-filled situations, and if you are emotionally unstable, you could snap and ruin a relationship. It is crucial to reach out to other leaders for advice and help in managing your hectic life. By talking to people who are going through similar things, it helps you realize you're not alone.

—*Taylor Anne Adams, Wake Forest University senior, involved in Greek life, student government, and the dining commission*

The leader is the person everyone is looking up to, and if they show weakness or instability, the entire group will be affected and be unsure of the group's ability to perform and feel vulnerable. The leader has to be the rock for the group—she has to keep her emotions in check so the group doesn't have to.

—*Kelly Albanir, Cornell University sophomore, involved in the pre-orientation service trip, Cornell ambassadors, and women's crew team*

A leader can bring down a team or staff if they do not have their emotions in check. It is okay to have a bad day as long as you let people know that you are having one. This helps people understand the mind-set that the leader is in when making decisions.

—*Miranda Baker, California State University-Chico senior, involved in residence life and the pre-law society*

As a PhD student in biomedical science, I am constantly dealing with failed experiments and hypotheses. To help manage my emotions, I try to remember that adversity is part of the training; graduate degrees don't come without bruises.

—*Cody Rutledge, University of Illinois at Chicago graduate student, involved in the student-run free clinic and as a tutor*

References

Center for Conflict Dynamics. (2013). *Hot Buttons*. http://www.conflictdynamics.org/products/cdp/hb/index.php

McCauley, C. D., & Van Velsor, E. (Eds.). (2003). *The Center for Creative Leadership handbook of leadership development*. San Francisco, CA: Jossey-Bass.

Peck, M. S. (2003). *The road less traveled: A new psychology of love, traditional values and spiritual growth* (timeless ed.). New York, NY: Touchstone.

Whetten, D. A., & Cameron, K. S. (2010). *Developing management skills* (8th ed.). Upper Saddle River, NJ: Prentice Hall.

Yukl, G. (2010). *Leadership in organizations* (7th ed.). Upper Saddle River, NJ: Prentice Hall.

Reflection Questions

- Who in your life best exemplifies the capacity of emotional self-control? How so?

- When have you seen a leader, coach, or educator lose emotional self-control? How did others react? How did it affect the person's ability to influence others?

- What stressors are you navigating in your daily life? Where do you experience them, and how do you and others react?

- What are your hot buttons and who or what triggers them the most? How might you react in an emotionally intelligent way the next time this occurs?

Chapter 5 Authenticity

Being transparent and trustworthy. **Authenticity is about developing credibility, being transparent, and aligning words with actions. Emotionally intelligent leaders live their values and present themselves and their motives in an open and honest manner.**

You likely can pinpoint an experience in your life in which you lost trust in someone (e.g., a best friend, coworker, coach, teacher, supervisor). The person said he or she would do one thing but did another, did not share the whole truth, or did not act genuinely. This experience probably changed your perception of the person, and maybe even your relationship with him or her.

You might be wondering why a chapter on authenticity begins with a discussion on inauthenticity. In reality, it takes just *one* inauthentic or untrustworthy act for someone to lose credibility. Michael Josephson said, "We judge ourselves by our best intentions and most noble deeds but we will be judged by our worst act."

Trustworthiness is something we must work hard to gain. Our integrity and character are among our most valuable, and fragile, possessions. Although this is important for everyone to consider, it is even more important for people who wish to influence others and engage in leadership. People look up to, want to work with, and follow those whom they believe are trustworthy and authentic.

Being authentic means knowing what you stand for. You know your values, and you align your actions with your values. Further, you include others in this process by communicating your values and discussing why they are important. Some may call this *living out loud.* When a person consistently lives out loud, others notice and are drawn in. People recognize authentic leaders are leading for the right reasons and are concerned about others more than their own recognition and success. This empowers and encourages others to live and lead authentically (George, 2007).

Aligning Values, Words, and Actions

Early conceptions of authenticity can be traced back to the quote "To thine own self be true" (Avolio & Gardner, 2005). Authenticity is a tall order. Authenticity calls for consistency across a person's values, words, and actions (Yukl, 2010). This is much easier said than done. One reason why is the inner work you must do to identify the values and principles central to who you are. You also have to do the "outer work" of aligning those values with how you act and behave. How well do your actions and behaviors align with your core values and principles? How do you let your values be seen by others in action? By communicating these values, it becomes clearer to others what you stand for and why you behave the way you do. This helps to build trust and credibility, and it serves as a foundation for developing healthy relationships.

> Your values are your foundation. It doesn't matter what you build or who you're leading—it all begins with what you value.
> —*Bo Renner, University of Arkansas senior, involved in student government and Razorback Foundation*

Authenticity also takes courage and dedication. It takes courage to know yourself well enough to choose the right path, which often is more difficult and time consuming than the "quick and easy" wrong path. Further, authenticity requires doing so in all aspects of your life—not just when you are in a specific situation or with certain people. The courage to be authentic could show itself in voicing an opinion that is different than the opinion of others or standing for something you believe strongly about. Being authentic may entail going against the grain and publicly expressing your beliefs and values.

> Authenticity means trusting in yourself, so others can trust in you.
> —*Samantha Lyons, University of Michigan sophomore, involved in a community service fraternity, running club, and the club sports council*

Because authenticity is so complex, it does not develop overnight; rather, authenticity is an ongoing process. Bill George (2007), author of *True North: Discover Your Authentic Leadership*, discusses this journey as continuously headed toward your true north. In this journey, your values and principles serve as an internal compass to help keep you on the path toward authenticity. If you use external forces as your guide, it is easy to get off course or lack clarity in your direction.

You have probably heard the phrase "going with your gut feeling." This refers to an intuitive feeling as to what you should do or what you should avoid. Scientific evidence supports the value of this gut feeling (Goleman, Boyatzis, & McKee, 2002). Our brain continually engages in learning processes. The brain "soaks up life's lessons to better prepare us for the next time we face a similar challenge, uncertainty, or decision point" (Goleman et al., 2002, p. 44). The emotional brain then sends these judgments to our gut, alerting us whether something feels right. Attunement to these messages requires an acute consciousness of self, with particular attention to the capacity of emotional self-perception (see chapter 3 on emotional self-perception).

Building Trustworthiness

One benefit of authenticity is that it helps build credibility and trustworthiness. Following through on commitments, which is a way of demonstrating authenticity, is a key step. A basic example of this is if you say you are going to complete a task, follow through on your word. If you say you will call someone, make sure you do so. Perhaps more difficult is to say "Yes" only to requests you can complete with excellence, and graciously say "No" to tasks you cannot prioritize. Many of us are accustomed to saying "Yes," which often helps us gain new opportunities, achieve recognition for our work, and grow as leaders. As important as this is, we must also know how and when to say "No" so that we don't overpromise and underdeliver. Can you think of a coach, teacher, supervisor, or coworker who struggles with this?

Another way to build trustworthiness is to allow yourself to be open, vulnerable, and genuine with others. In his bestselling book *Five Dysfunctions of a Team*, Patrick Lencioni (2002) identifies five dysfunctions that lead to team failure. The first of the five dysfunctions is an absence of trust. Trust is the backbone of any functioning group, and without it, a group cannot authentically engage with each other and, in some cases, a group may fail to reach its goals. When trust is in place, group members can also be vulnerable, which is a necessity for groups and teams. When we are vulnerable with others (e.g., being open, admitting mistakes, and revealing weaknesses), we facilitate more authentic relationships among group members.

Allowing yourself to be vulnerable in a group involves exposing your flaws and admitting you are not perfect. Yes, striving for excellence is important, but focusing on perfection prevents opportunities for growth, hinders one's ability to connect with others, and can negatively affect a group's process. Thus, rather than viewing vulnerability as weakness, which society often does, vulnerability can be a powerful leadership asset. Brené Brown (2012), author of *Daring Greatly: How the Courage to Be Vulnerable Transforms the Way We Live, Love, Parent, and Lead*, writes:

> Vulnerability is the birthplace of love, belonging, joy, courage, empathy, and creativity. It is the source of hope, empathy, accountability, and authenticity. If we want greater clarity in our purpose

or deeper and more meaningful spiritual lives, vulnerability is the path. (p. 33)

How much of your authentic self do you allow others to see? Do you have barriers that prevent you from being authentic and opening up to individuals and in groups? Allowing yourself to be vulnerable helps build trustworthiness.

> There is no such thing as a perfect leader. Everyone has their quirks, and being an authentic leader means recognizing and owning these idiosyncrasies and using them in a positive way to better the group.
>
> —*Karly Oberski, Central Michigan University senior, involved in a leadership organization, honor society, student government association, and health organizations*

Authentic Leadership

Avolio and Gardner (2005), prominent scholars on the topic of authentic leadership, distinguish between the concepts of *authenticity* and *authentic leadership*. Authenticity, as highlighted previously, is more intrapersonal (within you) because it is all about you—how you align your actions with your values and being true to who you are. Authentic *leadership*, however, emphasizes developing authentic relationships with others, which is more interpersonal in nature, recognizing "all leadership is relational at its core" (Avolio & Gardner, 2005, p. 332). Authenticity is a prerequisite for trusting relationships.

Think back to the scenario at the beginning of this chapter when you considered a situation in which you lost trust in someone. The person's inauthenticity affected more than just him- or herself; it affected the relationship with the other person and possibly even other relationships or organizational outcomes. As such, authentic leadership is central to emotionally intelligent leadership.

Student Voices

Values are the underlying direction of leadership. Values define the *how* through which leadership can be accomplished. Without values, leadership is directionless.

—*Stephen Roth, The Ohio State University graduate student, involved in Greek life and as a teaching assistant, university ambassador, and student leadership advocate*

Know what you stand for and, more importantly, what you do *not* stand for. A leader's authenticity will always be tested; it's important to always remain grounded in what you believe. Your authenticity is all you have.

—*Ryan O'Donnell, North Carolina State University junior, involved in service learning and a leadership organization, and is* CEO *and cofounder of a nonprofit organization*

If a leader doesn't believe in what they're doing, why would their followers listen? A leader needs to have a strong moral core behind everything they do.

—*Alexander Lyubomirsky, University of Maryland junior, involved in a business fraternity, an a cappella group, a student judiciary board, and as a resident assistant*

Authenticity means vulnerability when it comes to leadership. When you are able to admit that you are fallible and don't always have the answer, you will open up infinite doors to innovation with your team.

—*Gregory Rokisky II, Michigan State University senior, involved in the residence hall association and food services*

References

Avolio, B. J., & Gardner, W. L. (2005). Authentic leadership development: Getting to the root of positive forms of leadership. *Leadership Quarterly*, *16*, 315–338.

Brown, B. (2012). *Daring greatly: How the courage to be vulnerable transforms the way we live, love, parent, and lead*. New York, NY: Penguin.

George, B. (2007). *True north: Discover your authentic leadership*. San Francisco, CA: Jossey-Bass.

Goleman, D., Boyatzis, R., & McKee, A. (2002). *Primal leadership: Learning to lead with emotional intelligence*. Boston, MA: Harvard Business School Press.

Lencioni, P. (2002). *The five dysfunctions of a team: A leadership fable*. San Francisco, CA: Jossey-Bass.

Yukl, G. (2010). *Leadership in organizations* (7th ed.). Upper Saddle River, NJ: Prentice Hall.

Reflection Questions

- What are some of the core values and principles that guide your actions?

- In what situations has your authenticity been compromised? Why you do think this was the case? What was the outcome?

- In what ways have you demonstrated vulnerability in a group? Did it help or hinder the group process?

- What are some of the commitments in your life you need to continue to say "Yes" to? What might you need to say "No" to?

- What is one practice you can implement in your everyday life to enhance your authenticity?

Chapter 6 Healthy Self-Esteem

Having a balanced sense of self. **Healthy self-esteem is about balancing confidence in your abilities with humility. Emotionally intelligent leaders are resilient and remain confident when faced with setbacks and challenges.**

Unlike many emotionally intelligent leadership (EIL) capacities, healthy self-esteem is fairly abstract. Simple definitions of self-esteem include feeling good about yourself and having a sense of who you are. Healthy self-esteem, in the context of EIL, means balancing humility with a belief in your abilities. This means you know yourself well enough to stand up for what you believe in while understanding that you may not know it all and need to create space for the thoughts, opinions, and values of others. Whom do you know who best exemplifies this capacity?

> If someone has too much confidence, they lose focus of the goals in the project and of the team. Empathy and interpersonal skills are necessary to balance personal confidence.
> —*Aime Szymanski, John Carroll University senior, involved in Greek life, honor societies, and club lacrosse*

The "healthy" part of this capacity means that you hold yourself in check. Self-confidence, believing in yourself and your abilities, is a key ingredient of self-esteem. Too much self-confidence, though, can lead to arrogance, which is problematic on a number of fronts. This is why humility is key. Just like a chef needs a balance of seasonings in preparing a dish, we too need to keep a balance of our sense of self. Another essential ingredient of healthy self-esteem is resilience, which entails recovering quickly from setbacks. Thus, demonstrating EIL often requires a healthy and balanced sense of self, self-efficacy, and resilience.

A Healthy Balance

Imagine having an emotional bank account (Covey, 1989). Every time something goes well, a deposit is made into the account. When something happens that causes you pain, a withdrawal is made. Healthy self-esteem exists when your bank account is comfortably above the minimum balance. Clearly this level is different for each of us, which is one of the great challenges of understanding self-esteem.

Think of a time when you were part of a group that made you feel great just by being a member (e.g., athletic team, work team, class project, student organization). When you are in the presence of others who make you feel good, you get a deposit in the emotional bank account, and your self-esteem benefits. You are more likely to feel good about yourself and develop a sense of your capabilities. You believe you can accomplish what you want, you are competent, and you appreciate your skills and abilities. You also know your limitations and can accept when you have not done something well. When your emotional bank account is at a healthy level, it gives you a safety net as well as a foundation upon which to build. Using this metaphor of an emotional bank account—and even trying to visualize it—can help you be more aware of yourself, believe in yourself, and feel more competent and confident. You can draw on this awareness when you need to boost your self-esteem.

Just as important as strengthening your self-esteem is learning how to keep yourself in check. This is why we assert "healthy" as part of this capacity. Although showing appreciation and recognition is important, overuse can lead to exaggerated egos and an unrealistic view of hard work and success (Twenge, 2006).

> Be independent and brave without being overbearing or prideful. This is important because all leaders must also at some point be followers.
> —*Hannah E. Stone, Loyola Marymount University junior, involved in student government*

If any of us continuously hear praise without critique, we might experience feelings of superiority. This can lead to demeaning, exploiting, or dismissing others; narcissism; and disappointment or even depression from unmet expectations (Baumeister, Campbell, Krueger, & Vohs, 2003; Twenge, 2006). Clearly, we need to strike a balance between feeling good and confident about ourselves while still being humble and open to the opinions, perspectives, and thoughts of others.

Self-Efficacy

Bandura (1993) defined self-efficacy as "people's beliefs about their capabilities to exercise control over their own level of functioning and over events that affect their lives" (p. 118). Self-efficacy affects a person's thought processes, motivation, feelings about others, and decision making. As a result, the connection between self-efficacy and healthy self-esteem is clear. For people to believe in themselves, to have confidence in their abilities, to have the courage to stand up for their convictions, and to have the comfort to connect with others, they must have a sense of self-efficacy. Bandura (1993) identified four factors that can positively influence one's self-efficacy, and when applied to the context of leadership these are:

1. successful past leadership experiences,
2. observation of others demonstrating successful leadership,
3. affirmation and encouragement from others in one's leadership abilities, and
4. positive moods and emotions.

These factors suggest that our self-efficacy can develop over time through gaining experience, observing and learning from others, interacting with people who support and encourage you, and demonstrating positive emotions.

Research on college student leadership development demonstrates that an individual's belief in oneself matters, and this changes over time. In a large national study, college seniors demonstrated greater confidence in their ability to engage in specific leadership behaviors than they did before they were in college (Dugan & Komives, 2007). An interesting outcome of the study was that men had stronger self-efficacy for leadership than women. This means that self-efficacy may be an area for women in college to focus more attention on in their leadership development.

> To help boost my self-esteem I try to hang out with people with positive energy who I know will always bring me up and never put me down.
> — *Hannah Sullivan, high school sophomore from Beachwood, Ohio, involved in student council and lacrosse*

Healthy self-esteem can support you in making a big decision about what you want to accomplish as an individual or as a member of a group. This is when we see self-efficacy in action. You may feel more motivated to work with others on a task that is challenging and important because you believe you can make a difference. You have the confidence to take risks. This state of mind sets up the active side of self-esteem—providing energy, inner strength, and power (Avolio & Luthans, 2006).

Resilience

While writing the first edition of this book, Marcy's seven-year-old daughter said, "You know Mommy, it's really important to love yourself first." When asked why, she said, "Well, you know, if you don't love yourself first, then how can you love anyone else?" Sometimes the wisdom of a child is overwhelming. She identified one of the first steps of developing leadership—believing in and loving yourself. This is a step toward developing resilience as well.

> Recognize not only what you excel at, but maybe more importantly recognize where your shortcomings lie. This is crucial to strong leadership because it allows the team to focus on areas that should be improved.
> —*TJ Fisher, Rollins College senior, involved in an honor society, Greek life, an allies program, and as a tour guide*

Now, Marcy's daughter is in her early teenage years and has begun to demonstrate healthy self-esteem. The first really bad grade she received, after years of doing all "A" work in school, was a shock to her system, yet she bounced back quickly. In middle school, she encountered peer pressure and strong social pressures. Watching her daughter manage setbacks, arguments, and challenging friendships earlier in life caused Marcy to rethink her own experiences. Today's challenges are greater and more intense, which means that it is all the more important to learn how to rebound when things are not going well. Being resilient means knowing how to bounce back from challenges. The old cliché of picking yourself up after falling down has tremendous relevance to leadership.

Knowing who you are helps you navigate pressure, push through adversity, and recover from mistakes. Research has found that healthy self-esteem contributes to better performance in school, getting along with other people, and respecting the rights of others (Baumeister et al., 2003). Likewise, developing healthy self-esteem at an early age helps you become more resilient as an adult. We all know that falling down is inevitable—it is what you do once you are down that matters. We must learn how to come back from these experiences better, stronger, and even smarter. Resilience is a cornerstone of healthy self-esteem. It also plays an important role in optimism and authenticity, two other EIL capacities (Avolio & Gardner, 2005; see chapters 5 and 9).

Giving In Versus Giving Up

Much like developing leadership, acquiring and sustaining healthy self-esteem is an ongoing, lifelong process. Unlike an innate talent, healthy self-esteem is both a mind-set and a skill set because you feel and demonstrate it daily, if not hourly. From a difficult conversation with a friend or parent to a hard class, demonstrating healthy self-esteem can be a challenge. In many ways, healthy self-esteem requires grit, which is a powerful combination of perseverance and passion for a long-term goal (Duckworth & Peterson, 2007).

Because of constant pressures, consider the reality of maintaining healthy self-esteem. Grit reflects how difficult it can be to face the demands upon us. To develop healthy self-esteem, realize that when you face a challenge, you may need to take the necessary time to identify how important the challenge is to overcome. What if the challenge is so great that your sense of self will be damaged? Or is the situation one in which you may just have to endure a lousy day?

These questions get at the overarching question of "When is enough, enough?" Certain situations or setbacks may cause us to draw down our emotional bank accounts, perhaps even to the point where we have a negative balance. Another option may be that we accept that we have to give in to a challenge, acknowledging we cannot be everything to everyone. This may translate into a short-term loss for the long-term gain of maintaining your healthy self-esteem. In this case, giving in is a conscious choice based on counsel from trusted friends, reflection, and analysis. This is different than giving up, which is often more about quitting or taking the easy way out. Giving in, ironically, can also make a deposit in our emotional bank account—saying "No" can be an affirmative statement of who we are.

Scott has struggled with this notion of not saying "No" much of his adult life; as a result he takes on too much, which affects his health, his family life, his relationships with friends, and at times, his overall mental state. The source of *why* Scott feels compelled to say "Yes" is an interesting concept for exploration. Is it simply his love for the work? Or, is it to please others? Does it help him feel accepted and prove his worth to receive external validation from others? These are some big questions that he has been working on for years, and although he is better at saying "No," he still has work to do in this realm. This all revolves around the challenges of healthy self-esteem.

Student Voices

To have healthy self-esteem means to believe in yourself and believe that you are capable of the task at hand. It also means being willing to recognize where improvements need to be made, even if that is within yourself.

—*Rebecca Stelfox, Arizona State University senior, involved in Teach for America and Greek life*

Self-esteem is often misinterpreted with arrogance. If one is confident, they are humble and do not shy away from critique, which is key for leadership. Even though a leader is given a higher standard, there is always room for improvement.

—*David Tassone, Loyola Marymount University sophomore, involved in student government and a religious organization, and as a resident advisor and track coach*

Confidence is a double-edged sword; on one side you want to be confident in what you do, but too confident can turn off fellow team members.

—*Ty McTigue, John Carroll University senior, involved in orientation, tutoring, and Greek life*

When I need a boost in my self-esteem I try to calm myself down and focus on one achievement of which I'm most proud; that, or simply relive happy memories.

—*Rachel Elson, high school junior from Shaker Heights, Ohio, involved in rugby, soccer, and the student group on race relations*

References

Avolio, B. J., & Gardner, W. L. (2005). Authentic leadership development: Getting to the root of positive forms of leadership. *Leadership Quarterly*, *16*, 315–338.

Avolio, B. J., & Luthans, F. (2006). *The high-impact leader*. New York, NY: McGraw-Hill.

Bandura, A. (1993). Perceived self-efficacy in cognitive development and functioning. *Educational Psychologist*, *28*(2), 117–148.

Baumeister, R., Campbell, J., Krueger, J., & Vohs, K. (2003). Does high self esteem cause better performance, interpersonal success, happiness, or healthier lifestyles? *Psychological Science in the Public Interest*, *4*(1), 1–44.

Covey, S. (1989). *The seven habits of highly effective people: Powerful lessons in personal change*. New York, NY: Fireside.

Duckworth, A. L., & Peterson, C. (2007). Grit: Perseverance and passion for long-term goals. *Journal of Personality and Social Psychology*, *92*(6), 1087–1101.

Dugan, J. P., & Komives, S. R. (2007). *Developing leadership capacity in college students: Findings from a national study*. A Report from the Multi-Institutional Study of Leadership. College Park, MD: National Clearinghouse for Leadership Programs.

Twenge, J. M. (2006). *Generation me: Why today's young Americans are more confident, assertive, and entitled—and more miserable than ever before*. New York, NY: Free Press.

Reflection Questions

- When do you feel at your best? Think about the context—what you are doing—and who you are with.

- Think about someone you know who seems to demonstrate healthy self-esteem. How do you know? How do you feel when you are with this person?

- In general, how resilient are you? How well do you bounce back from setbacks?

- When have you said "No" or stopped doing something and felt like your decision gave you a boost of confidence?

- In what ways have you recently made a deposit to *your* emotional bank account?

Chapter 7 Flexibility

Being open and adaptive to change. **Flexibility is about adapting your approach and style based on changing circumstances. Emotionally intelligent leaders seek input and feedback from others and adjust accordingly.**

Change Is Inevitable

Think about your life ten years ago. How were you different? How was the world different? We would guess that both have changed considerably. In reality, we all need to embrace change on some level. We need to adapt, grow, and develop. The same can be said of our larger world, and of us. This is one reason why flexibility is so important.

Philip Crosby, a businessman and management author, said, "If anything is certain, it is that change is certain. The world we are planning for today will not exist in this form tomorrow." As Crosby suggests, little is certain in our world, and society is becoming increasingly complex. Increased globalization paired with technological advancements, demographic shifts, and economic and social forces lead to a world that is ever changing. Organizations that become stagnant lose their relevance and effectiveness—and in many cases, fail.

Consider a quote from the Chinese text *Tao Te Ching*: "Whatever is flexible and flowing will tend to grow, whatever is rigid and blocked will wither and die." This perspective applies to both people and organizations. People and organizations that are rigid will fail to adapt to the world around them. As such, leadership requires an openness to possibilities and new ways of working to be successful and effective. We can't stress enough the importance of flexibility and adaptability in leadership. Daniel Goleman (2001), an author and scholar on emotional intelligence, sums this up for us: "If there is any single competence our present times call for, it is *adaptability*" (p. 35).

Being Open and Adaptive to Change

Flexibility is about being responsive to changing situations. EIL involves changing and modifying behavior, ideas, and approaches based on the situation. Although we may be more naturally drawn to certain leadership styles, EIL promotes flexibility in our approach as needed. One of the best-known leadership theories, situational leadership, stresses the importance of being adaptive when leading (Blanchard, Zigarmi, & Nelson, 1993). The theory emphasizes learning how to be flexible based on the needs of the group and your assessment of the context in relation to your own abilities, knowledge, and skills.

> A leader who can't make changes in him- or herself can't make changes in the world.
>
> —*Tracey Riley, Loyola University Chicago senior, involved in honor societies, crisis hotline, and as a research assistant*

Consider a student who takes charge of a group project in class because she feels her classmates are not as motivated as she is. How she decides to lead the group depends on her classmates' perceived motivation and what the assignment requires. This same approach, however, may not work in her community service project team where everyone is equally motivated and everyone wants to have a say in the work and contribute to the project. If the student does not adapt her approach based on the situation, she will be less effective in the community service group.

As the previous example suggests, flexibility is about more than just changing your leadership style. It also means being open to different ideas, perspectives, and opinions. Being flexible from the standpoint of EIL means being willing to change your mind based on new information or experiences. In fact, EIL demands that we continually examine situations to broaden our perspective and see our environment through different lenses. Can you think of a coach, teacher, supervisor, or coworker who exemplifies this capacity? How does it affect others?

Be Flexible ... to a Point

Oftentimes, people mistake flexibility for being wishy-washy or two-faced. U.S. President Thomas Jefferson provided great guidance when he said, "In matters of style, swim with the current; in matters of principle, stand like a rock." Your ability to swim in many currents will expand your horizons, introduce you to a wide variety of perspectives, and lead you to experience life to the fullest with greater ease and satisfaction. Balancing flexibility with your principles, however, means that you remain rooted in your values and your ethical principles, which will earn you greater respect and credibility. When rooted in principle and conviction, embracing flexibility in your leadership style helps you further your purpose and the values for which you or your organization stands.

> Flexibility is about seeing the big picture and not getting caught up in the extraneous details.
> —*Katelyn Park, Clemson University senior, involved in Greek life, a leadership honors society, a pre-med honors society, and on a research team*

Another way of looking at this is keeping the purpose or mission central to what you do, while allowing for flexibility in *how* this mission or purpose can be accomplished. Imagine you are in charge of planning homecoming festivities, and you have a vision in mind for the various events. You have a committee eager to be a part of the event, and the committee members have a number of ideas that you hadn't considered. You will have to consider where you need to hold true to the mission and purpose of homecoming, and where you can let go of some of your ideas to be more flexible in considering and implementing others' ideas. By being too flexible you could risk losing your vision, and by being too rigid you could lose committee members and their good ideas and energy.

Importance of Feedback

Being flexible also means creating opportunities for input and feedback. Our knowledge and perspective is limited to our own experiences, identities, and ways in which we make meaning of situations. Other people's perspectives, ideas, and opinions can provide additional insight into a situation or our behavior. Take, for example, attending a student organization meeting with a friend. After the meeting, your friend may be upset about something that happened in the meeting that you didn't notice. Through conversation, you start to think about the meeting differently based on her perspective.

> Every leader has two options. Continue to lead as though you're doing everything right, or gain feedback from those who see you lead. Every good leader knows that feedback is your friend.
>
> —*Bo Renner, University of Arkansas senior, involved in student government and Razorback Foundation*

This is just one example of how we all experience situations differently and notice some aspects or details more than others. Being flexible means being open to seeing and understanding what others experience and see. This requires both consciousness of self and the ability to display empathy (see chapter 2 on consciousness of self and chapter 12 on displaying empathy).

When we seek out others' perspectives and learn from them, we develop a more holistic view of the situation. This results in more informed decisions and solutions. In addition, gathering input and ideas from other people helps them feel more involved in the process of leadership. When others feel their ideas and feedback are taken into consideration, they are more likely to support the final outcome or decision. Even if their course of action is not always chosen, they will likely be more invested in the process because they felt they were heard.

Student Voices

Leadership is about a goal and the people. While there must be a common goal, it is important for a good leader to be flexible and adaptable to the people he or she is leading.

—*Vanessa Ruvalcaba, California State University, Monterey Bay recent graduate, involved in an LGBT organization*

Flexibility helps you lead with care and diligence. Adaptability enables a leader to be open to others' ideas and to adapt to the changes created by those ideas.

—*Adam Odomore, Texas State University junior, involved in a volunteer organization, leadership organizations, and a Black men's organization*

Things will go wrong no matter how hard you try. If you aren't prepared to alter your plans to the world around you, the world will move on without you.

—*Alexander Lyubomirsky, University of Maryland junior, involved in a business fraternity, an a cappella group, a student judiciary board, and as a resident assistant*

Before, during, and after every meeting, my team knows they are encouraged to give feedback. Our team will only grow if our best ideas are put forward, and listening to everyone brings us closer to our goal.

—*Ryan O'Donnell, North Carolina State University junior, involved in service learning and a leadership organization*, *and is* CEO *and cofounder of a nonprofit organization*

References

Blanchard, K. H., Zigarmi, D., & Nelson, R. B. (1993). Situational leadership after 25 years: A retrospective. *Journal of Leadership Studies*, *1*(1), 21–36.

Goleman, D. (2001). An EI-based theory of performance. In C. Cherniss & D. Goleman (Eds.), *The emotionally intelligent workplace: How to select for, measure, and improve emotional intelligence in individuals, groups, and organizations* (pp. 27–44). San Francisco, CA: Jossey-Bass.

Reflection Questions

- Think about yourself over the past three to five years. What worked for you in the past that doesn't work today? What is it about you that has changed?

- What core principles or values ground you and keep you steady during times of change?

- How open are you to others' ideas? How well do you integrate other people's ideas into your own?

- How do you gather different perspectives from group members on an issue?

- When you have an opportunity to make an important decision, how often do you ask other people for their ideas?

Chapter 8 Optimism

Having a positive outlook. **Optimism is about setting a positive tone for the future. Emotionally intelligent leaders use optimism to foster hope and generate energy.**

Optimism is a word with which everyone is familiar. Within the context of emotionally intelligent leadership (EIL), optimism means demonstrating a healthy and favorable outlook, fostering hope, and setting a positive tone for the future. Optimism is a powerful force that, when demonstrated effectively, is contagious. In our experience, we find many people overlook this capacity or do not think it is an essential part of leadership. Research, however, supports our position. In fact, studies suggest optimism is an important element of, and provides a link between, emotional intelligence *and* leadership (Avolio & Luthans, 2006; Bar On, 2010).

> When optimism is streaming through an organization, there is no end to the possibilities that could be accomplished. There is thought, creativity, relaxation, and, most of all, fun.
>
> —*Anonymous, Michigan Technological University sophomore, involved in the university programming board, fraternity, job/internship, and as a volunteer*

Generating Energy

Think about a friend of yours who can easily energize a group. His or her presence can make the difference between an average night or an *amazing* night out with friends. What is it about this person that fosters these feelings in others? Is it his or her sense of humor or outlook on life? Perhaps he or she breathes life into the conversation or makes others feel good. Now, think about your friend who is perceived as a bit of a downer. Or, think of the person on social media who is always making comments that bring others down. He or she struggles to put things in a positive light. Which person would you rather have as a leader, parent, coach, teammate, or teacher?

> There is a sense that things, if you keep positive and optimistic about what can be done, do work out.
> —*Hillary Rodham Clinton, former U.S. Secretary of State*

Leadership scholar Warren Bennis (2000) said the following of optimism: "Every exemplary leader that I have met has what seems to be an unwarranted degree of optimism—and that helps generate the energy and commitment necessary to achieve results" (p. 61). It is likely you have seen or felt something similar in your own experiences. Emotionally intelligent leaders are optimistic and set a positive tone.

Think about your own experiences. Have you had the opportunity to be part of a group or team with coaches, mentors, advisors, teammates, or teachers who set the right tone? If so, it's likely they had the ability to bring people together and inspire them through their positive outlook. Often just setting foot into that teacher's classroom, reflecting back on a conversation with your mentor, or working with that coach made you feel good about what you were doing. Setting a positive tone makes work more engaging and enjoyable for everyone involved.

Optimism in Action

So what tone do *you* set when leading others? Do people enjoy working with you? Do people choose to spend time with you? Are you a positive influence on the organization or an energy drain?

These questions can help you identify your attitude and abilities as they relate to optimism. According to research,

> Optimists interpret both successes and failures differently than pessimists. Optimists ... do not take failures personally ... They view failure as a temporary setback and only in this situation. On the other hand, pessimists make the opposite attributions—they take failures personally, as long lasting, and generalize to everything they do.
>
> (Avolio & Luthans, 2006, p. 153)

Your ability to assess what is in and out of your control, navigate the challenges that come with leading others, and maintain a positive outlook in the face of challenge will set you apart.

> As a leader, all eyes are on you and so you must constantly maintain a positive attitude in order to maximize results. When leading others, sometimes you have to see beyond the outcome and appreciate the growth that took place to get there.
>
> —*Jasmine Ramon, Alfred University sophomore, involved in women's leadership academy, women's soccer, and a diversity organization*

In our work with students, we have noticed two key points about optimism. First, students with leadership responsibilities are often so consumed with the task at hand that they forget they are responsible for setting the emotional tone of the group. For instance, if they do not have a positive outlook about the work or seem unhappy and disinterested, it is unlikely others will feel the same. Students who have the ability to display genuine enthusiasm for the work of the group (and its individual members) are at an advantage when it comes to leadership.

Second, students often miss important opportunities to demonstrate optimism at work, in student groups, during internships, on the athletic field, and in the classroom. For instance, simply thanking people for their good work reflects optimism.

Seeing the good in a group and commenting on it publicly is an important skill. These are influential and easy steps to take in setting the tone and recognizing the good work of others, but displaying optimism isn't always easy. It can be especially challenging to demonstrate optimism during difficult situations, because this is often when people in the group need it the most. Leadership involves delivering bad news, addressing conflicts, challenging unethical behaviors, and making tough decisions. Even in these difficult situations, you can exude a measured level of optimism to help the group move forward and see that a tough decision will help in the long run.

Realistic Optimism

Now, we all know leadership is not all tulips, warm fuzzies, and chocolate bars. In fact, the literature on leadership is out of balance and often overly positive (Kellerman, 2004). Leadership can be dangerous, risky, and extremely difficult, yet that side of leadership is seldom revealed. Leadership is rarely free from conflict, challenge, and stress. Being optimistic does not mean that you are oblivious to real issues, blind to the challenges facing the group, or insincerely positive. In fact, emotionally intelligent leadership often means being the catalyst for the conflict. In concert with other EIL capacities like managing conflict, analyzing the group, and assessing the environment, emotionally intelligent

> If a student leader lacks optimism, it can be like an airborne virus, infecting everyone else around them because negativity spreads quickly. This could break down the morale of the whole group because you feed off each other to be successful in reaching goals.
>
> *—Jade Sydney Alexis Kendle, University of North Texas senior, involved in Greek life, the progressive Black student organization, and as a campus life ambassador*

leaders see complexities and problems as inherent in all organizations. While sometimes this means actively working to overcome them, at other times it may mean making the tough decision. Realistic optimism helps us approach situations and relationships in a different manner by which we understand, and even expect, that challenges are part of the work. Thus, you are better prepared to engage with others to move through or past them without dwelling on the negatives. Realistic optimism means you see the possibilities without overlooking the realities.

Realistic optimism results in helping others see a range of possibilities in difficult situations. For example, viewing conflict as a catalyst for a new idea or a way to deepen or strengthen a relationship rather than the *end* of a relationship or a huge setback is a manifestation of optimism. Realistic optimism helps us identify gaps or weaknesses (because we know they are there) and transform them into learning opportunities or assets. Optimists practice the habit of learning when something does not happen as expected. When this occurs, the inner dialogue goes something like this, "Well, that stinks. Now what can I learn from it?" An optimist challenges others to do the same when they face setbacks. By doing so, resiliency builds. Optimism equips us to face obstacles with energy and the ability to bounce back, learn, and move forward.

Emotions Are Contagious

Research supports the idea that emotions, both positive and negative, are contagious. For example, a concept called *mood linkage* explains instances in which the mood or outlook of an individual or small group affects the entire organization (Williams, 2005). This concept can work for or against you.

> Optimism is the key to a great leader! No one wants to be a member of an organization that is led by someone who is not passionate and excited about its success.
> —*Brooke Pankau, Rollins College senior, involved in student government association, student life committee, and as a peer mentor*

Think of an organization or sports team with great success. It is likely the team members are on a collective high. One person's positivity feeds off of others, and this is a powerful force. Now think back to a time when you were in an organization in which the leader or a small group of influential individuals were negative toward the organization. You may have heard comments such as "Things used to be so much better"; "This organization is going nowhere"; "I don't care anymore—I couldn't care less." If left unattended or unaddressed, these comments are toxic and destructive.

In looking at these two scenarios, the former is certainly favorable. We all know, though, that the organizations and groups in which we are involved will not always experience success. Every organization has issues. A key question is: Are you willing to be part of the solution? Addressing this question from the perspective of EIL means understanding the challenges, seeing opportunities, and being willing to work toward a resolution. In effect, this means we recognize the challenges but choose our attitude (Lundin, Paul, & Christensen, 2000). By choosing our attitude, we take responsibility for our attitude and make adjustments as needed. If we succumb to pessimism, we see how negative energy sucks the life out of an organization—similar to a Dementor in the *Harry Potter* series. We are reminded of the words of Remus Lupin to Harry, "Dementors are among the foulest creatures that walk this earth ... They drain peace, hope, and happiness out of the air around them ... Get too near a Dementor and every good feeling, every happy memory will be sucked out of you" (Rowling, 1999, p. 187). Ever known a person like that?

Tough Questions …

So what type of leader are you? Do people in your organization view you as optimistic or pessimistic? Do people enjoy being around you? Are everyday challenges huge issues that get you down, or do you navigate these hurdles with ease and grace? What would people who know you best say? Are you able to portray optimism even when delivering bad news or when times are tough?

From a leadership perspective, Bass (2008) found "successful leaders have revealed a more optimistic view of themselves and the world around them than have nonleaders and those leaders who have tried and failed" (p. 182). Some people seem innately optimistic and foster a sense of hope; others tend to look on the negative side. If you find it hard to see the positive or to be optimistic, try spending time with people who breathe energy and life into the organization. Likewise, pay close attention to how others react to you when you are in a negative space. Remember to *choose your attitude* (Lundin et al., 2000). If this is a struggle for you (and you are not alone), begin to develop that part of you that appreciates people and looks for possibilities. From there, practice verbalizing a positive outlook. As you focus on optimism, you will begin to shift your thinking more toward the positive. Although optimism may not become your greatest strength, it *can* become an asset as you work with others to take your leadership abilities to the next level.

Student Voices

In the history of armed conflict, we hear all about "morale of the troops." It is such an important factor that several major battles have been lost to forces of smaller size because the troop morale was low. We have to be positive! If the leader shows lack of support or little enthusiasm, how can he or she effectively delegate?

—*Reynaldo Muniz III, Jamestown Community College sophomore, involved in student senate, the faculty student association board, and as a student ambassador*

If a leader lacks optimism, the productivity of a group slows drastically. If the leader isn't passionate about what they're leading, their group members will feel it and most will reflect with disengagement and apathy.

—*Gregory Rokisky II, Michigan State University senior, involved in the residence hall association*

Leaders should have a clear view of the goal that they want to reach. If they lack the optimism or confidence in their ability to reach those goals, how can they expect their followers to believe in them?

—*Nicole Olson, Central Michigan University graduate student, involved in Greek life, a leadership organization, and a health organization*

A leader without optimism creates animosity and a hostile environment. Those who work with the leader can lose interest in things they once were interested in and often find the leader unapproachable, which encroaches on the foundation of a working group.

—*Katelyn Park, Clemson University senior, involved in Greek life, a leadership honors society, a pre-med honors society, and on a research team*

References

Avolio, B. J., & Luthans, F. (2006). *The high impact leader*. New York, NY: McGraw-Hill.

Bar-On, R. (2010). *A broad definition of emotional-social intelligence according to the Bar-On model*. http://www.reuvenbaron.org/bar-on-model/essay.php?i=3#optimisim

Bass, B. (2008). *The Bass handbook of leadership: Theory, research and managerial applications* (4th ed.). New York, NY: Free Press.

Bennis, W. (2000). *Managing the dream*. Cambridge, MA: Perseus.

Kellerman, B. (2004). *Bad leadership: What it is, how it happens, why it matters*. Boston, MA: Harvard Business School Press.

Lundin, S. C., Paul, H., & Christensen, J. (2000). *Fish! A remarkable way to boost morale and improve results*. New York, NY: Hyperion.

Rowling, J. K. (1999). *Harry Potter and the prisoner of Azkaban*. New York, NY: Scholastic.

Williams, C. (2005). *Management* (3rd ed.). Mason, OH: South-Western College Publishing.

Reflection Questions

- Emotionally intelligent leadership helps us capitalize on untapped potential, unleash energy, adapt, and communicate a better future. Who does this well within your circle of friends?

- When have you seen optimism affect organizations? How about a lack of optimism?

- What specific behaviors do you employ to breathe life and energy into your organization(s)?

- When might optimism become a detriment to a leader?

- On a scale of 1 to 10, with 10 being highest, how would you rate the energy within your primary student organization? On what basis do you make this rating?

- Why is it important to *choose your attitude* as a leader? When is this difficult to do? Are you skilled at doing so?

Chapter 9 Initiative

Taking action. Initiative means being a self-starter and being motivated to take the first step. Emotionally intelligent leaders are ready to take action, demonstrate interest, and capitalize on opportunities.

A Broader Perspective

What if Abraham Lincoln had not taken the initiative to tackle the issue of slavery in the United States? What if he had decided that it was simply too controversial to take on? All of us would be different people, living in a different world. Leaders such as Mahatma Gandhi, Nelson Mandela, Gloria Steinem, Susan B. Anthony, Martin Luther King Jr., Golda Meir, Mikhail Gorbachev, Mother Teresa, and Lech Walesa sparked change in their countries and the world. In the words of Kouzes and Posner (2007), "Leaders go first," and each of these individuals took initiative, even when faced with seemingly insurmountable odds.

Initiative is powerful. The individuals listed not only saw that the world could be different but also *took action*. Thankfully, we do not have to be world leaders to take initiative. Every day people take initiative in large and small ways. The key is that we see and we act without being prompted to do so. In his video *The Power of Vision* (1991), futurist Joel Barker suggests, "Vision without action is merely a dream. Action without vision just passes time. Vision with action changes the world."

Reasons for *Not* Taking Action

In our work with students, we have witnessed a great deal of untapped potential—individuals who could have made a difference and accomplished their goals, but for one reason or another chose not to. This is a problem for many reasons. Organizations, groups, campuses, and society must continue to grow to stay relevant and best serve their purposes. Initiative is about being proactive to bring about change by showing interest, being a self-starter, and taking action.

Based on our experience, we see four primary reasons that students fail to take action in various contexts (e.g., groups in class, student organizations, workgroups in their place of business, athletic teams): fear of failure, apathy, popularity, and the inability to manage conflict.

> A teacher once told us, "If you want to do something great, put yourself in a position to fail," and it's really stuck with me. He meant that if you don't take any risks and don't put yourself out there, sure, you won't be embarrassed, but you also won't accomplish anything. Fear of failure is very counterproductive because it doesn't necessarily protect you from failure, but it does impede your success.
> —*Naomi Grant, high school junior from Beachwood, Ohio, involved in student council, school newspaper, yearbook, and Model UN*

Fear of Failure

In each and every organization there are problems. Whether it is a fraternity that hazes its new members, a student government bogged down by gridlock, or a new organization trying to recruit members and develop traditions, leadership can move an organization past its challenges and unhealthy behaviors. This only happens, however, when someone takes the first step and speaks out against the norm or takes an unknown path. This can be risky business. Thus, initiative takes courage because leadership can be dangerous. Simply look at the names mentioned earlier in this chapter and you will see what we mean. Think about your own organizations. The thought of losing friends, not being cool, looking foolish, or not succeeding are enough to stop many people from taking initiative. Fear of failure causes many of us to stall, hold off, or choose a safer path. EIL helps us take that first, difficult step.

Apathy

Another reason for inaction is the amount of work and energy it takes to begin the work toward change. Many of us may simply think we do not have the energy or time to take on new efforts, and, as a result, problems persist. Every organization, group, and workplace has members who are apathetic, unmotivated, and even lazy. However, when formal leaders are also that way, a dangerous and unhealthy dynamic occurs, and the organization can quickly spiral downward. Tackling tough issues or starting something new takes a great deal of time and mental energy. Focusing too much on the cost rather than the potential benefits is one of the many reasons why apathy may keep us from taking initiative.

Popularity

A third reason for inaction is popularity. It may be deemed unpopular to take a stand against hazing, eating disorders, alcohol or drug abuse, or cheating. The fear of being outcast by others we care about is a powerful force. As a result, many follow the herd and put up with unhealthy practices, behaviors, and even personal habits to the detriment of the larger group. Each one of us has fallen victim to this reality and wish we could go back and alter our approach. However, conforming and maintaining popularity among peers is a major driver of behavior, no matter how old we are. We see this in athletics, politics, business, and social groups. When was the last time you failed to take a stand because it was the safer option? When was the last time you opted out of doing something different because you were afraid of what other people would think? How did that affect the organization?

Inability to Manage Conflict

A final reason for not taking action is a fear of conflict. As we discuss in the chapter on managing conflict (see chapter 19), the goal of maintaining harmony is a strong driver of behavior. This is especially true if you do not feel like you are skilled at navigating difficult conversations or extended periods of conflict. Cliché as it may sound, the fear of "opening a can of worms" or "discussing the elephant in the room" is real. This fear surrounds us, in our families, organizations, friendships, and workplaces—really in all human social systems. The downside of inaction is that when problems persist, self-doubt festers and relationships and groups become divided. In a leadership role, we may be perceived as weak and ineffective because a certain faction would like the conflict addressed, and by choosing to do nothing, that faction becomes disheartened, disengaged, or apathetic. For all these reasons, and more, EIL advocates taking initiative.

Hallmarks of Initiative

So what does a healthy level of initiative look like? In our work, five major actions stand out. People who take initiative actively engage, are confident in their abilities and beliefs, consistently innovate, secure support, and maintain focus. Each of these actions is like a lever for change. They don't necessarily have to follow one another because sometimes just one action is sufficient.

First, taking initiative means seeing a gap or opportunity and acting to fill it. For example, within a student organization you may see an opportunity to grow your organization and actively seek ways to enhance the group. In your personal life, you may see a friend with an eating disorder and try to help. Taking initiative means you are actively engaged; you see an opportunity to act and do so. Taking action and pushing through challenges are key components of initiative.

> A spoken word is nothing but sound. A spoken word with initiative behind it is a powerful tool that can turn any thought into reality.
> —*Rebecca Clements, Central Michigan University junior, involved in the honors program, and as a leader advancement scholar and leadership safari guide*

A second hallmark of taking initiative is having the confidence to stand up for what is right and work through the issues that may follow. Emotionally intelligent leaders know they can navigate change and make their group, their community, or the world a better place. We have great respect for those we know who have tackled problematic traditions in organizations such as: sexism, racism, homophobia, hazing, and alcohol or drug abuse. We have seen students completely transform their organizations into stronger and more inclusive organizations that make a significant impact on campus. We have seen students work with a friend through difficult personal issues, even when it meant taking a personal risk themselves. Taking initiative requires confidence in your ideas and in your ability to make a difference.

A third hallmark of those with initiative is they are innovative and often seem to be ahead of the curve. Think about Steve Jobs and his career—for years, he was on the cutting edge of multiple industries. Throughout his career he took risks, and much of the time (but not all) it paid off. Now, we do not assert that Jobs was perfect by any measure, and by many accounts, he lacked emotional intelligence, but he did exemplify innovation. Successful designers, engineers, programmers, video game architects, artists, and musicians are often innovating. Think of someone you know who is creative or an entrepreneurial thinker. They often see problems as opportunities.

Our fourth hallmark is about securing support. Knowing that there are inherent obstacles ahead, taking initiative includes reaching out to mentors, trusted advisors, peers, and others who can serve as sources of support. By doing so, you gain emotional

> Without initiative, no leader would be where they are today. Initiative is the backbone to a successful leader.
> —*Katherine Du Pont, University of Oregon recent graduate, involved in female associated students, student recreation center advisory board, and as an athletics commissioner*

support and identify valuable resources to help you climb over, crawl under, or work through barriers in an effective, ethical, and entrepreneurial manner. This is certainly challenging, so seeking out people who have a similar vision and can help support you makes a significant difference.

A fifth hallmark of initiative is to focus. Initiative requires us to set a goal and stay focused on the end product. With this focus, we can remain highly motivated and not easily distracted until we have met our goal. This means we may get up early, stay late, or even view everything through the lens of meeting our goals and the goals of the group or organization. In this way, initiative is directly linked to the capacity of achievement (see chapter 10). Initiative is about being the spark, and achievement is about following through.

A Door Waiting to Be Opened

We love the following quote from our friend Denny Roberts (2007): "To envision is to have a picture of how something might be. It is having a different idea in our head about how a particular circumstance might be if it could be improved" (p. 110). This vision may be about you, your group or organization, a cause, or your community. Regardless, EIL means demonstrating your interests, finding or creating opportunities, and acting upon them. This means staying focused. Whether it is a problem in the current culture or an idea that can take an organization or even yourself to the next level, you act. Hearing objections does not distract an individual with a healthy level of initiative.

Initiative means that when you discover a closed door, you see it as just that—a closed door, waiting to be opened. Of course this can be taken to an unhealthy extreme, so it is important to turn to others for feedback, guidance, and support. After all, it is just as important to know when not to take initiative, hold off, take a more measured approach, or look for opportunities elsewhere.

Student Voices

Initiative is important for any student leader, but especially for students at large universities because opportunities are much more difficult to locate, strictly due to the breadth of the school. In order to change the world, students have to be inspired and diligent in finding the opportunities to support their choices.

—*Alex W. Bugg, University of Kentucky junior, involved in agricultural biotechnology club, student government association, and as a college of agriculture ambassador*

A student who has too much initiative may preemptively agree to take on new leadership roles or tasks without realizing the toll they will take on him or her. It is important for a student to always be "hungry" for a challenge or for trying something new, but he or she should make sure it is feasible with his or her lifestyle and schedule first.

—*Erica Bilodeau, Castleton State College recent graduate, involved in student government association, student orientation, residence life, and a student activities intern*

There's a difference between having initiative and being a pest. I've found that a good gauge is to read the feedback you're getting. If someone is excited to be talking to you, engaging you, and asking questions about your ideas, then you know this is someone you want to continue working with. On the opposite end, if you're receiving terse responses that cut to the chase, generally it's time to direct your efforts elsewhere.

—Tess Duncan, Elon University senior, involved in student government association, Greek life, and freshmen summer experience

---

Initiative is a must because it drives change. Healthy initiative involves making sure it does not conflict with your ability to readily adapt to the unavoidable truth that leadership involves people, and people are not predictable. Too much initiative can tunnel your vision and prevent you from taking a detour when the original route was quite obviously obstructed.

—JoAnna Adkisson, Belmont University graduate student, involved in Greek life, dance marathon, a diversity committee, and as a student ambassador and admissions student recruiter

References

Barker, J. (1991). *The power of vision* (VHS). United States: Starthrower Distribution.

Kouzes, J., & Posner, B. (2007). *The leadership challenge: How to keep getting extraordinary things done in organizations* (4th ed.). San Francisco, CA: Jossey-Bass.

Roberts, D. (2007). *Deeper learning in leadership: Helping college students find the potential within.* San Francisco, CA: Jossey-Bass.

Reflection Questions

- Which of the four causes of inaction have you displayed? Which do you see as most common?

- When have you embodied the five hallmarks of initiative? Which might you further develop?

- What does initiative taken to an extreme look like? Can it hurt an organization? If so, how?

- How do leaders spark initiative in others?

- Who do you turn to as a source of support? How has this helped when leading others?

Chapter 10 Achievement

Striving for excellence. **Achievement is about setting high personal standards and getting results. Emotionally intelligent leaders strive to improve and are motivated by an internal drive to succeed.**

Striving for Excellence

Within the framework of emotionally intelligent leadership (EIL), achievement means striving for excellence. Research demonstrates those who are achievement oriented "get satisfaction from succeeding at tasks. They have self-imposed standards of excellence" (Bass, 2008, p. 179). Perhaps you have a friend who is achievement oriented and goes above and beyond what is expected. This passion for achievement is a fuel that drives behavior. Do you have it? If so, in what areas of life do you feel most motivated to achieve your goals? Are you perceived as an individual continually taking your knowledge, skills, and abilities to the next level, or are you seen as someone who is okay with the status quo? These questions have important ramifications for you as you think about leading others.

> A student has a healthy level of achievement when all others around them stand just as tall. Teamwork would be at an all-time high.
>
> *—Cleyton Cavallaro, Michigan Technological University sophomore, involved in Greek life and broomball*

Getting to Flow

Achievement begins with examining what you feel passionate about. Achieving results becomes effortless when we truly want to excel in a given domain. Passion is an energy source unlike any other and, at its best, often leads to a psychological state called *flow* (Csikszentmihalyi, 1990). In essence, you experience flow when you are so immersed in an activity that you lose track of time and the world around you. Flow is associated with feelings of confidence, excitement, and positive energy. What is this activity for you? For some, it is dancing or writing; for others, it is playing sports, serving in the community, or playing a musical instrument. When you love an activity, it is easy to enter the state of flow.

Flow fosters achievement. People who intrinsically value what they are working on do not necessarily need to set formal goals or establish high standards for themselves. These ingredients are already there. Do you think it is difficult for Beyoncé to motivate herself to sing, act, or dance? Perhaps some days, but many would agree that she is here on earth to entertain. It is easy to perform above and beyond expectations or the competition when you are in a state of flow.

To connect this concept to you, think about your past academic year. Which subjects did you enjoy the most? Math? English? Leadership? In these classes, you were probably more successful, did not doubt your abilities, and did not even notice the time passing because the subject or the activities just clicked for you. Achievement in these classes was probably not a challenge. These classes probably took less effort and time than those classes you did not enjoy. Although we cannot always be in a state of flow, finding ways to capitalize on our passions and strengths is an efficient and effective way to excellence.

Practicing Achievement

When engaging in activities you love, it is not difficult to set high standards and tap into your internal drive to succeed. Because leadership is difficult, taking on the responsibilities and the risks of leadership is made easier when you love what you are doing. Finding your passion, however, may take some time. Getting involved by joining organizations or clubs, getting an internship or job, serving on a board, or volunteering in the community helps you develop as a leader. Research shows holding a formal leadership role is positively associated with developing student leadership capacity (Haber, Allen, Facca, & Shankman, 2012; Haber & Komives, 2009; Posner & Rosenberger, 1997). By affiliating with organizations for which you have a passion, you will be intrinsically motivated. This means you are naturally driven to perform in that realm. No one needs to motivate you to work hard or be committed to your responsibilities.

In addition to joining organizations, try taking on additional responsibilities and practice your leadership. For example, Scott currently serves on three boards, and he views these experiences as opportunities to *practice*. The organizations have very different objectives, goals, and members, and each has a unique set of challenges that must be addressed. Each provides perfect opportunities for learning and growth. Like other capacities, achievement takes a great deal of deliberate practice (Ericsson, Krampe, & Tesch-Römer, 1993). As mentioned at the beginning of the book, deliberate practice involves intentionally working on developing yourself through continuous, focused, and ongoing effort and attention. For instance, if you struggle to encourage a group of people, are you practicing your skills of motivation and learning how to improve yourself? Are you seeking feedback from others on how you can improve and grow?

> A dream doesn't become a reality through magic; it takes sweat, determination and hard work.
> —*Colin Powell, former U.S. Secretary of State*

Repetition and ongoing work is a key part of deliberate practice. Research suggests it takes ten years or ten thousand hours of deliberate practice to achieve expertise in a given domain (Ericsson et al., 1993). Unlike athletes or musicians, aspiring leaders often have to coach themselves. Thus, setting goals, tracking progress, seeking feedback, and reflecting are all key behaviors that support achievement.

A critical thing to remember as a student leader is that we're students. When someone is too focused on achievement sometimes you miss the amazing learning opportunities that can come from failing.
—*Tess Duncan, Elon University senior, involved in student government association, Greek life, and freshmen summer experience*

Do What You Love, but Beware

When we are doing what we love, we are motivated to succeed, feel energized by the work itself, and feel inspired. Mark Twain said, "Make your vocation your vacation." All too often people do not take the time to truly discover their passion and core purpose, which makes achievement more challenging. With passion and deliberate practice as a foundation, you have an amazing starting point.

We would like to offer two cautions. First, be in tune with the source of your motivation. We have worked with students whose achievement orientation is for personal gain rather than to better an organization or cause. This results in a loss of trust and influence. Second, we have witnessed students diminish their impact because they were *too* achievement oriented. Individuals who are too focused on this capacity may lose sight of the bigger picture or have unrealistic expectations and diminish their effectiveness with individuals or the group.

A student leader is too focused on achievement when, at the end of their term as a leader, there is no one adequately prepared to replace them. An effective leader is equally as focused on fostering the leadership and growth of others as they are on having a successful organization.
—*Kathryn Appelbaum, University of South Carolina, works as a radio station manager*

Remember, leadership is about influencing others to

achieve results—*not doing everything yourself*. If you are consistently the only person working above and beyond expectations, you may be focused on the wrong objective and may not be providing opportunity for others to contribute. One objective of leadership is getting others to work above and beyond *with* you. Otherwise, you are not leading anything; you are just doing a lot of stuff, and no one is following or working alongside you.

Student Voices

A student leader is too focused on achievement when they are constantly stressed out and base their self-worth on what they are achieving.

—*Miranda Baker, California State University, Chico senior, involved in residence life and the pre-law society*

They say money can't buy happiness, and I think achievement works the same way. Once your drive for achievement is so high that it cuts out other priorities, responsibilities, and relationships, it's a problem.

—*Hannah Buehler, University of Maryland junior, involved in professional engineering fraternity and student government association*

A healthy level of achievement is similar to a well-balanced meal. You're focused on the main course, but there are other ingredients that help bring it all together.

—*Ken Clar, John Carroll University senior, involved in Greek life, Relay for Life, campus ministry, and as a tour guide*

A student has a healthy level of achievement when failure does not paralyze him or her, but rather sparks a deep desire to improve.

—*Eden B. Bunch, Texas State University graduate student, involved in graduate student affairs council and in national student affairs and academic advising association*

References

Bass, B. (2008). *The Bass handbook of leadership: Theory, research and managerial applications* (4th ed.). New York, NY: Free Press.

Csikszentmihalyi, M. (1990). *Flow: The psychology of optimal experience*. New York, NY: Harper & Row.

Ericsson, K. A., Krampe, R. Th., & Tesch-Römer, C. (1993). The role of deliberate practice in the acquisition of expert performance. *Psychological Review*, *100*(3), 363–406.

Haber, P., Allen, S. J., Facca, T., & Shankman, M. L. (2012). College students' emotionally intelligent leadership: An examination of differences by student organization involvement and formal leadership roles. *International Journal of Leadership Studies*, *7*(2), 246–265.

Haber, P., & Komives, S. R. (2009). Predicting the individual values of the social change model of leadership development: The role of college students' leadership and involvement experiences. *Journal of Leadership Education*, *7*(3), 123–156.

Posner, B. Z., & Rosenberger, J. (1997). Effective orientation advisors are also leaders. *NASPA Journal*, *35*(1), 46–56.

Reflection Questions

- What activities, topics, sports, or hobbies bring you into the psychological state of flow?

- Do others perceive you as achievement oriented? What are the positive and negative ramifications of these perceptions?

- What happens when a leader is focused on personal gain instead of leading for the benefit of the organization?

- What achievement(s) in your life are you most proud of?

Part Two: Consciousness of Others

Chapter 11 Consciousness of Others

Demonstrating emotionally intelligent leadership involves awareness of the abilities, emotions, and perceptions of others. Consciousness of others involves intentionally working with and influencing individuals and groups to bring about positive change.

Leadership Is a Team Effort

As Susan Komives emphasized in the foreword of this book, leadership is not a solitary act. By nature, leadership is interpersonal. Call them followers, members, peers, or constituents, leadership is a relational process that involves the interpersonal dynamic of self in relation to others.

By being conscious of other people's abilities, emotions, and perceptions, you can better inspire, connect with, work with, and influence others. One traditional view of leadership is the Great Man or heroic leader who is solely responsible for leadership. This image of leadership is outdated, ineffective, and simply not accurate. In her TED Talk, Dr. Quyen Nguyen, a physician and professor of surgery, discusses this concept and suggests:

> Our society loves to romanticize the idea of the single, solo inventor who, working late in the lab one night, makes an earthshaking discovery, and voila, overnight everything's changed. That's a very appealing picture; however, it's just not true. Medicine today is a team sport … Successful innovation is not a single breakthrough. It is not a sprint. It is not an event for the solo runner. Successful innovation is a team sport, it's a relay race.
>
> (Nguyen, 2011)

This quote extends beyond the field of medicine. Today, we see how leadership in many different fields and disciplines is a team effort and rarely a solo act.

> You cannot have leadership without collaboration. If a leader is unwilling to collaborate, there will be many conflicts, brick walls will be hit, and no progress will be made. Can we really call that leadership?
>
> —*Melissa Looby, Rollins College junior, involved in service organizations, a religious organization, and as a student diplomat and ambassador*

An example of this comes from Paige's leadership role of being head of the prom committee in high school. At the time, she viewed leadership as being the person in charge. Beyond telling the committee members what to do, she did not engage her peers in the planning process and did not solicit ideas or empower group members. At the time, she was confused because more than half of the committee stopped coming to the meetings. She jokes about it now, saying, "It wasn't really a prom committee. *I* was the prom committee." Looking back, the planning process was stressful, and the end product, the prom, had considerable room for improvement. If Paige had been more in tune with her committee members and used the capacities outlined in this part of the book, both the process and the outcome would have likely been more successful and enjoyable.

We all know the saying "Two heads are better than one." We strongly believe this to be true, and the power and potential of leadership increase when working with others. We also believe leadership takes considerable attention, skill, and practice. Awareness of the people with whom we are working is incredibly important for the success of the leadership process and for achieving desired end results. The nine capacities within consciousness of others encompass skills, abilities, and other characteristics that are essential when working with others.

> None of us is as smart as all of us.
>
> —*Ken Blanchard, leadership author*

The Interpersonal Dimension of Leadership

> Everyone brings strengths to the table, and it is important to utilize them to run an effective organization.
> —*Elizabeth Mills, University of Iowa sophomore, involved in the residence hall association, student government, an honors fraternity, and a political organization*

Early leadership researchers focused solely on the leader without acknowledging other people (e.g., followers, group members, collaborators, employees). This early research was limited in scope and left much to be explained. In recent years, research has not only recognized but also elevated the important role that others play in the leadership process.

As such, consciousness of others is the second facet of EIL. This facet emphasizes the importance of others' abilities, emotions, and perceptions. No matter your position or role in a group, consciousness of others involves getting to know people below the surface and working with them to achieve desired results. EIL includes being emotionally in tune with others and inspiring action. Likewise, consciousness of others challenges us to build teams, coach others through change, and consistently understand the perspectives and background of the group.

A focus on and investment in others is vital and serves as a necessary foundation to effectively enact the nine capacities of consciousness of others:

1. Displaying empathy
2. Inspiring others
3. Coaching others
4. Capitalizing on difference
5. Developing relationships
6. Building teams
7. Demonstrating citizenship
8. Managing conflict
9. Facilitating change

An example of how these capacities work together can be seen through the lens of being a captain of an athletic team. To be successful, for instance, Kate, who is captain of her basketball team, needs to have an acute understanding of herself as well as a set of skills related to working with others. At times, she will need to display empathy as she manages conflict and helps the students on the team through difficult times. She will need to inspire others as she facilitates some type of change and keep them motivated. If her peers view her as a model citizen, she will have more credibility. Finally, if she has spent time developing relationships, it is likely this investment will pay off during difficult times with her teammates as well as contribute positively to a well-functioning team and successful season.

> I see the best leaders as those who are willing to embrace the concept of we, not me.
> —*Alex Myers, John Carroll University junior, involved in a health organization, intramural sports, and as a tour guide and teaching assistant*

This example demonstrates the importance of the different capacities and how they work in conjunction with one another. Through demonstrating consciousness of others and effectively enacting the related capacities, we have the ability to move a group forward and bring about change. The chapters to follow examine each of the consciousness of others capacities in more depth.

Student Voices

No single individual is capable of covering all the bases and thinking outside all the boxes, so working with members can boost the success and efficiency of a group.

—*William Lehman, Michigan Technological University senior, involved in Greek life, a LGBT pride group, an a cappella group, and a psychology association*

I often ask people who tend to be a little quieter what they think; they tend to have perspectives that not everyone had thought of.

—*Kimberly Johnson, Central Michigan University sophomore, involved in the fashion association and a Black student organization*

When I was starting a mentoring program, I had this image in my head of what I wanted the program to be, and it sometimes caused me to shoot down a good idea without truly considering its possibilities. Luckily, I was working with a strong group of women who brought this to my attention. Through collaboration, one person's good idea can snowball with another good idea and before you know it, the good idea has turned into a great program through the collaboration of many.

—*Dianne Mattar, Alfred University senior, involved in a ski team, outdoor club, mentoring program, honor society, engineering organizations, women's leadership academy, and as an orientation guide*

It is impossible for one person to know everything about anything. It is inevitable, when working with another person, that a new idea or outlook or approach to a situation will come up that someone never would have thought of on their own.

— *Sophie Foxman, high school senior from Toronto, Ontario, involved in yearbook and a regional youth group*

Reference

Nguyen, Q. (2011, October). *Quyen Nguyen: Color-coded surgery* [Video file]. http://www.ted.com/talks/quyen_nguyen_color_coded_surgery.html

Reflection Questions

- What has been your best group experience? What made it so positive?

- What has been your worst group experience? What made it so negative?

- Which of the nine capacities in this section are you most interested in? Which might you need to focus on?

- What happens if a leader lacks the ability to truly engage and work with others?

- Can you think of a personal example similar to Paige's example of leading the prom committee? How have you developed or grown since then?

Chapter 12 Displaying Empathy

Being emotionally in tune with others. **Empathy is about perceiving and addressing the emotions of others. Emotionally intelligent leaders place a high value on the feelings of others and respond to their emotional cues.**

Displaying empathy requires placing a high value on emotions and being emotionally in tune with others (Bar-On, 2007; Buckingham & Clifton, 2001; Lawrence, Shaw, Baker, Baron-Cohen, & David, 2004). Closely tied to emotional intelligence, displaying empathy is one of the most powerful and difficult EIL capacities to learn and practice. Being empathetic helps you build healthy relationships, manage difficult situations, and develop trust. To be empathetic, you must know what you are feeling (emotional self-perception) to be able to acknowledge and identify what others may be feeling. Empathy involves being perceptive and sensitive to what you see, hear, and think.

As you can see, displaying empathy is tied to many other capacities of EIL. As a point of clarification, empathy is different from sympathy. *Sympathy* means "putting yourself in another person's place but retaining your own perspective and still using your own standard of judgment" (Komives, Lucas, & McMahon, 2007, p. 171).

> As a leader I believe you should have empathy towards others because it shows you care; nobody likes surrounding themselves around a mean leader.
>
> —*Michelle Munoz, Berkeley College recent graduate, involved in work study and as an orientation leader*

Simply put, sympathy involves pity, while empathy requires understanding.

It's a Process

A key aspect of displaying empathy is social perspective taking. Social perspective taking is the ability to see another person's point of view and to recognize his or her thoughts and feelings. Research has found that college students' ability to effectively engage in social perspective taking contributed to a stronger sense of self as well as greater ability to work effectively with others (Dugan, Bohle, Woelker, & Cooney, 2014). The question is: How do we do this? Social perspective taking involves some key behaviors:

- being able to "listen to and absorb information skillfully,
- recognizing that other people's views of the situations may be different from yours,
- understanding that other people's assumptions may be and should be different from yours, and
- understanding and accepting the limitations of your own point of view." (McCauley & Van Velsor, 2003, p. 369)

We think it is important to discuss this four-step process in greater depth. As you read the following paragraphs, think about a difficult conversation you have had in recent months with a family member, friend, classmate, team member, coach, or coworker. In which of these areas did you do well and where could you have improved? This type of reflection will help you develop and grow as you work to better display empathy.

Listening

One way to move empathy from an intangible idea to a practical skill is to think about empathy in the context of communication. For example, when you listen empathetically, you hear people's words using your ears, eyes, and heart. In other words, you hear what is said along with how those words are spoken. You listen for the tone used and the emotions that may exist behind the words. You notice body language. You focus on what they are saying, not on what you want them to be saying or what you want to say back. Many people are familiar with Stephen Covey's quote, "Seek first to understand, then be understood."

> Empathy is important because as a leader you have to understand your audience. You can't connect with people and inspire them to do things if they don't feel like you understand them or care.
> —*Marek Bruckner, Trinity University junior, involved in Greek life and volunteer action committee*

Although simple in concept, empathetic listening is difficult to master. The first step is to slow down so that you can be tuned in and present with others. This can be difficult for even the most skilled communicators in the heat of a difficult conversation. Like many other capacities discussed throughout the book, this approach to listening requires deliberate practice.

Recognizing Difference

Once you have slowed down to learn the other person's perspective, you can begin to better understand how that person experienced a situation. This is important because each of us experiences the world in a different manner. We all have different histories, assumptions, backgrounds, and human characteristics that lead us to experience the world in different ways. Seeking to understand others' perspective does not mean you *agree* with them; it simply means that you *have an understanding* of their ideas from their vantage point.

A few suggestions are warranted to successfully navigate the challenges of understanding differing views. A basic suggestion ties these first two steps together, and that is to listen and not interrupt the other person. Along with this, if you focus on maintaining a slower pace to the conversation, you can more easily manage differences when they arise. When a conversation becomes heated, the pace increases, and this may increase the likelihood that we say something unintended. Be sure to ask clarifying questions so you are sure that you truly understand the other person's perspective. These questions should be phrased carefully so that they do not intensify or further divide.

Recognizing Assumptions

As you better understand the other person's perspective and discover differences, you may uncover a difference in assumptions as well. These differences may relate to values, expectations, and even goals. Perhaps you can even stretch to better understand *why* they hold their perspective. This is at the core of empathy. Assumptions about how things should be (according to your own perspective) can serve as a major source of misunderstanding. As each of us has experienced, differing assumptions are difficult to manage by themselves. When we add poor communication to the mix, we have a recipe for disaster. In part, displaying empathy is about navigating different assumptions while maintaining strong communication. You can take courses to help you explore this further. Likewise, you may have peers or mentors who excel in this type of communication. Watch and learn from them because we often learn the most through experience and from role models.

Understanding the Limitations of Your Point of View

Finally, be sure you explore the limitations of your own thinking and behavior. Knowing your own limitations strengthens your ability to display empathy. Seeing that you have limited points of view is challenging because ego and emotions *will* cloud your judgment and perspective. So, it is important to look within and explore what you may not see (your blind spots) or what you do not see fully because of bias, past experiences, or limited knowledge. Your willingness to examine your own limitations will diffuse a tense situation and help you identify with the other individual. Again, you may not agree, but you may examine the situation better because of a more empathetic approach.

Empathy in Action

Displaying empathy is not easy. As leadership scholar Bernard Bass (2008) suggests, "Leadership of a group depends, to some extent, on the leader's ability and motivation to estimate accurately the group's attitudes, motives and current level of effectiveness" (p. 130). Empathy involves placing a high value on the feelings of others, showing concern, and responding to their needs. You may feel empathetic, yet some might say that this capacity is in the eyes of the beholder. Empathy expressed by one person may not be perceived the same way by another. This means you have to practice your skills and learn how others think you display empathy. Ask for feedback from others you trust. Would they say you are empathetic? How good are you at listening empathetically? What are you communicating to others through your body language?

> When a leader lacks empathy, individuals in the group tend to get left behind because the leader doesn't try to put himself or herself in the individual's shoes.
>
> *—Nuo-Si Lei, University of British Columbia Okanagan junior, involved in campus life and the Southeast Asian club*

In addition, demonstrating empathy comes from your heart *and* your head. Empathy is not just about using logic to figure out the right words to say. Displaying empathy entails being sincere in what you are saying because you feel the other person's emotions too. Think about a difficult time in your life. Who did you feel was there for you? How did you know you had this person's support? What did this person do? We tend to respond better to others who show a genuine interest in us. Leaders who effectively display empathy are in a better position to truly connect and build lasting relationships with others.

Student Voices

Empathy is one of the most important abilities of a leader. Empathy, by my definition, is the ability to understand what people feel (and why they feel that way). Empathy is important for leaders because understanding the motivations of other people can only help the leader improve a team.

—*Anonymous, Massachusetts Institute of Technology senior, involved in an honor society, volunteer work, job/internship, and a religious organization*

In the short-term, a lack of empathy may be efficient but in the long-term, it will lead to lack of motivation and progress.

—*Aya Mimura, University of Michigan junior, involved in central student government, first-year experience, and as a resident advisor*

Having empathy allows a leader to check that the perception of what they are doing matches their intention. It is also a powerful insight to how to work with an individual.

—*Kacie Nice, Purdue University senior, involved in residence life, student newspaper, and student government*

When leaders lack empathy, it becomes highly difficult for them to collaborate with other members in the group. As leaders in our program, it was important for us to empathize because we were all different and this helped us understand each other and connect personally and collectively, therefore positively impacting our group.

—*Zabebah Mohamed, College of Staten Island - CUNY graduate student, involved in a leadership program*

References

Bar-On, R. (2007). The Bar-On model of emotional intelligence: A valid, robust and applicable EI model. *Organisations & People*, *14*, 27–34.

Bass, B. (2008). *The Bass handbook of leadership: Theory, research and managerial applications* (4th ed.). New York, NY: Free Press.

Buckingham, M., & Clifton, D. O. (2001). *Now discover your strengths*. New York, NY: Free Press.

Dugan, J. P., Bohle, C. W., Woelker, L. R., & Cooney, M. A. (2014). The role of social perspective-taking in developing students' leadership capacities. *Journal of Student Affairs Research and Practice*, *51*(1), 1–15.

Komives, S. R., Lucas, N., & McMahon, T. R. (2007). *Exploring leadership: For college students who want to make a difference* (2nd ed.). San Francisco, CA: Jossey-Bass.

Lawrence, E. J., Shaw, P., Baker, D., Baron-Cohen, S., & David, A. S. (2004). Measuring empathy: Reliability and validity of the Empathy Quotient. *Psychological Medicine*, *34*, 911–919.

McCauley, C. D., & Van Velsor, E. (Eds.). (2003). *The Center for Creative Leadership handbook of leadership development*. San Francisco, CA: Jossey-Bass.

Reflection Questions

- How important do you think empathy is to leadership? Would you consider it an essential skill? Why or why not?

- How has empathy (or the lack of it) affected past leader-follower relationships in your life?

- How would you rate yourself as a listener? Do you listen to understand or listen to respond?

- Which step(s) of the four-stage process for displaying empathy come naturally to you? Which step(s) are more difficult?

- What are the downsides of empathy? How might it be overused or even abused?

Chapter 13 Inspiring Others

Energizing individuals and groups. **Inspiration occurs when people are excited about a better future. Emotionally intelligent leaders foster feelings of enthusiasm and commitment to organizational mission, vision, and goals.**

Inspiring others is vital for demonstrating many other capacities of emotionally intelligent leadership (EIL). Often people name those leaders who are visionaries when asked about leaders whom they most admire. These are the individuals who capture your heart and create energy and excitement in groups of people. We know it when we see it, and we know it when we feel it; however, what "it" actually is can be challenging to describe or define. Like leadership, inspiration exists in the eye of the beholder (Bass, 2008). Someone who inspires one person is not necessarily inspirational to another (e.g., think presidential politics in the United States). Think about a coach who brought out the best in his or her team. Maybe you once were part of a group that accomplished great things beyond what any individual thought was possible. Have you ever faced a hardship and then someone said or did something that changed the situation for the better? In each of these instances, inspiration played a part.

The Challenge of Energizing Others

Most organizations, groups, and businesses benefit from a mission or vision statement to bring people together and create a common sense of direction. Pause for a moment. Can you name the mission statement of your favorite organization? We would guess no. These statements are often long, not very exciting, and lost in the shuffle of everyday activities.

Not only are these statements difficult to remember, they often do not effectively communicate why an organization exists. Why do we serve a purpose and why is that purpose exciting? The *why* often gets lost in the day-to-day actions of members, and leaders have the responsibility to keep people focused on the essential purpose of the work. According to Avolio (2005), inspiring leaders are "focused, and aligned around a common purpose, which they work to get others excited about and energized toward achieving. They are positively driven leaders who create a positive expectation for success in followers" (p. 196). While optimism clearly plays a part, inspiring others requires so much more. Energizing others is difficult work for a few basic reasons.

First, you may not see yourself as inspirational, yet as a leader, you are expected to generate energy, excitement, and commitment. Perhaps you are a quiet person who does not like the limelight. You will be happy to know that inspiration comes in many forms. The problem is that people often think of only one form: charisma. Being a charismatic leader, however, may not align with your self-concept. The good news is that inspirational leaders foster commitment in a number of ways, through their actions, use of emotion, strong relationships, and innovative ideas. So you do not need to be the person who can "fire up" the group like a motivational speaker or coach does. Instead you can inspire others through relationships or by consistently modeling citizenship.

> The most genuine way to inspire others is to be the most accurate representation of yourself at all times. It's when we try too hard to impress others or make an impact on them that things come off as unnatural or phony, causing us to be less inspiring to others.
>
> —*Alexandria Whittler, Loyola University Chicago sophomore, involved in the Black cultural center*

A second challenge associated with energizing others is that it can take a lot of energy out of you. Leadership scholar Bernard Bass (1990) suggested, "The inspirational leader has to have insight into what will be challenging to a follower and for what reasons" (p. 207). This can be an exhausting process. Not only do you have to manage your own emotions (emotional self-perception and emotional self-control), inspiring others means you are also expected to influence the emotional state of others. This is at the heart of emotional intelligence.

A third challenge with energizing others is that each of us is motivated in different ways. One task of leadership is to identify what motivates individuals and groups. For instance, one member of the student programming board may be motivated by working with bands while another gets excited about generating interest among the student body for a big event. The challenge is that to be effective, we need to spend time developing relationships with others so that we know what matters to them.

> To get people engaged and fired up, you have to address the passions and emotions of the group. People will be inspired if you can make them care.
>
> —*Amanda Werger, high school junior from Toronto, Ontario, involved in basketball, yearbook, a drama organization, and a regional youth group*

The good news is that each of these challenges can be managed with deliberate practice and effort. As we have mentioned elsewhere in the book, reflection and knowing yourself is a good starting point. Consider learning from someone whom you see as inspirational. What do they do? Another recommendation is to practice what you have identified as possible skills you have that inspire others. Then, surround yourself with mentors and peers who can provide you with feedback. Developing this capacity means taking these and other basic steps to inspiring others.

Practice Inspiration

In the introduction to this chapter we suggest that inspiring others can be accomplished through action, emotion, relationships, and ideas. It is important to reflect on which of these you bring. Regardless of context (e.g., a workplace, the classroom, an athletic team) the individual who models all four well will likely have greater influence. And each, as you will see, connects with other capacities of EIL.

1. *Action*: Leaders who model the way and live their values are a source of inspiration for others (Kouzes & Posner, 2012). Think of a friend who embodies the values she espouses. We would guess that her actions and the way she lives her life is a source of inspiration for you.
2. *Emotion*: If you have a genuine passion and enthusiasm for something (e.g., a hobby, cause, or organization), it is difficult to contain your energy. In fact, this energy influences your emotions and spreads to others, becoming a source of inspiration for some.
3. *Relationships*: A strong connection with others is the glue that holds organizations, teams, and groups together. Your ability to develop relationships will support your leadership efforts. Through building relationships, you can understand the people you are working with as peers or colleagues, not a random group of strangers. Your ability to develop meaningful relationships can inspire others.
4. *Ideas*: Your thoughts and ideas can be a source of inspiration. Innovative thinking is highly valued in many groups, and your ability to create and share novel ideas can inspire others, particularly if you can help them become invested in your ideas. Kouzes and Posner (2012) call this inspiring a shared vision, which can serve as a great source of motivation among a group. Many thought leaders have transformed our world and inspired millions through innovative ideas—think about Albert Einstein, W.E.B. DuBois, Margaret Mead, Thomas Edison, and Marie Curie.

> Inspiration starts in those you wish to inspire, not yourself. To get a group to be inspired you have to: know your audience, establish credibility, build a logical argument, and appeal to a group's emotions.
> *—Kevin Golla, University of North Dakota senior, involved in the campus wellness center*

Finally, one of the best ways to inspire others is to make them feel heard and valued. Emotionally intelligent leaders understand that inspiring others includes caring about them, their interests, their successes, and where they fit into the organization. It means showing that you understand what they need and want, which reflects the EIL capacity of displaying empathy. Although you cannot be all things to all people, you must know those whom you are leading and what makes them tick.

Be Intentional

Inspiration is crucial for effective leadership, and research suggests inspiration can be learned and developed. Zenger and Folkman (2013) conducted research on business executives who were striving to become inspirational. They found that executives made impressive strides in their ability to be inspirational, moving from below average to well above average.

This is good news for all of us. By being intentional, focusing our attention, and practicing, we can increase our ability to inspire others. Energize the group when they are down. Be the person who sparks enthusiasm. Stay in tune with your emotions and the emotions of the group. Paint a vivid vision for your organization and invite others to join in. Live your values. Keep others focused on the core purpose, and foster a sense of excitement for the work. We have seen many students successfully inspire others while fulfilling the mission and vision of their organizations, and we believe you can do the same. Remember that inspiration is often a by-product of the meaningful work being accomplished.

Likewise, inspiration must be combined with a number of the other capacities we have explored such as initiative and displaying empathy—inspiration alone will only get you so far.

Student Voices

When I first ran for an executive board position within the residence hall association, I lost, which I took extremely hard after spending weeks perfecting my speech and coming up with ideas to improve the position. Another open position was available, and the current executive board kept on encouraging me to apply, and it was because of their inspiration that I was able to stand in front of the general body again and win that election.

—*Mariah Geritano, Stony Brook University senior, involved in the residence hall association and the National Residence Hall Honorary*

In the student activities board (SAB) inspiration comes from getting people involved. Our goal is to know everyone on campus and to provide them with the best Cedar Crest experience possible. Inspiration comes from their years at Cedar Crest, and SAB knows that we make that experience much more fun.

—*Lindsay Amanda Faust, Cedar Crest College sophomore, involved in student activities board, the biology club, and as an orientation leader and academic services tutor*

My passion and love for my ethnicity helped me make my vision of creating a Jewish student union on campus a reality. This in turn played an important role in serving and inspiring other students on campus.

—*Tashiko Osiyo Del Toro Weinstein, Portland State University sophomore, involved in the resident housing association and the Jewish student union*

Inspiration happens when you can tap into individuals' emotions and the emotions of the group.

—*Michele Weiss, John Carroll University graduate student, involved in a women's advocacy group and works in the nonprofit sector*

References

Avolio, B. (2005). *Leadership development in balance*. Mahwah, NJ: Erlbaum.

Bass, B. (1990). *The Bass handbook of leadership: Theory, research and managerial applications* (3rd ed.). New York, NY: Free Press.

Bass, B. (2008). *The Bass handbook of leadership: Theory, research and managerial applications* (4th ed.). New York, NY: Free Press.

Kouzes, J., & Posner, B. (2012). *The leadership challenge: How to keep getting extraordinary things done in organizations* (5th ed.). San Francisco, CA: Jossey-Bass.

Zenger, J., & Folkman, J. (2013). What inspiring leaders do. *HBR Blog Network*. http://blogs.hbr.org/2013/06/what-inspiring-leaders-do/

Reflection Questions

- What qualities do you find in an inspirational leader? Ask your best friend the same question. Ask family members. Ask someone from a different background or culture. What are the similarities and differences?

- Do you consider yourself inspirational? If so, in what way(s)? If not, what have you learned in this chapter that could help you become more inspirational?

- How do you know what is inspiring to others? How do you know what others are looking for in a leader?

- How difficult is it for you to inspire others? Which of the three reasons mentioned in this chapter resonate with you?

- Of the four attributes of inspiration mentioned in the chapter (action, emotion, relationships, and ideas), which do you see as strengths? Which of these need more practice?

Chapter 14 Coaching Others

***Enhancing the skills and abilities of others.* Coaching is about helping others enhance their skills, talents, and abilities. Emotionally intelligent leaders know they cannot do everything themselves and create opportunities for others to develop.**

Developing Others

The emotionally intelligent leadership (EIL) capacity of coaching others reminds us that an essential responsibility of effective leadership is developing others. Great coaches are excellent teachers. They provide the challenge and support needed for people to work above and beyond their perceived limits. Many people associate coaching with athletics. Although this is certainly a common example of coaching and one with which many will resonate, coaching others is not limited to athletics or to having a formal, assigned title of coach.

Coaching is fundamentally about helping others grow and develop. From the perspective of EIL, coaching is a skill and ability that each one of us has, no matter our age. Even young kids in school coach each other. Here are a few examples:

- Jeff is a team captain and spends time building relationships with new team members. He takes the time to informally share what has worked for him.
- Shira is living in a residence hall on her campus for the second year in a row. During the first three weeks of class she helps other students on her floor adjust to their new environment.

- Jared is a young professional and spends time teaching new employees how to use the organization's online scheduling system.
- Rosa, the student government president, meets informally with a group of students interested in running for an office. She shares lessons learned, pitfalls to avoid, and techniques for running a successful campaign.
- Mei took on the position of group leader for an assignment in her graduate course and now has the responsibility of leading her classmates in achieving a challenging goal.
- Joelle serves as a math tutor helping classmates and first-year students in the lower level math classes.

In each of these examples, an individual is coaching another person with the expressed purpose of developing the other person's knowledge, skills, and abilities.

What Is Coaching?

Coaching is not one-directional. It involves mutual respect and reciprocity. Effective coaches care about and learn from those with whom they work. Often, they grow from the relationship as well. When a leader commits to coaching, an important shift takes place: leadership shifts from "me" to "we." Not only is there a recognition that leadership is about more than just one person, leadership is also about the future.

In the examples listed, helping someone learn a skill or acquire new knowledge is a priority. Coaching serves the essential function of creating a pipeline in which others become more proficient, adept, knowledgeable, and effective in their own leadership. Helping others develop skills and talents translates into greater capacity for not only that person, but also any group or organization to which they belong. This is often referred to as succession planning. When leaders help others develop, they are demonstrating other EIL capacities like achievement and citizenship, thus enabling others to maximize their contributions.

> It is important to give someone that extra push, backing up their beliefs, and building their confidence so they can instill their talents into the situation. This allows the leader to challenge the process and go outside of their comfort zone to grow.
>
> —*Victor Cimino, University of South Florida sophomore, involved in orientation, center for student involvement, Greek life, rock climbing team, and video game club*

Effective Coaching, Lasting Results

Effective coaching involves a focus on lasting results and relationships. Although leaders can be effective in the short term by selectively using leadership approaches that involve commanding others' attention and telling them what to do, these behaviors are not conducive to long-term results (Goleman, 2000). Long-term, sustainable results require more transformational approaches, of which coaching is a key component. Key coaching behaviors that yield greater results include

- willingness to initiate conversations and meaningful interactions;
- approaching coaching as a mutually beneficial relationship, not just a one-sided "telling" approach;
- focusing on specifics (e.g., certain constraining behaviors or attitudes) so that improvement and results are noticeable;
- demonstrating mutual respect (London, 2002).

Coaching others also entails helping others examine their "style, character, and how [they relate] to others over extended periods of time" (Avolio, 2005, p. 212). You do not have to be a formal coach to do this. In fact, effective coaching is often the result of good role modeling, and even friendship.

The Essential Skills

Just like an athletic coach helps his or her players develop their skills and draws out the best in the players, a leader does the same. One basic way of thinking about the coaching process is to see coaching in three parts: assessing, challenging, and supporting (McCauley & Van Velsor, 2003). In this respect, coaching requires us to learn about another person's knowledge, skills, and abilities and determine that person's strengths and limitations. On the basis of this assessment, coaching then consists of a healthy balance of challenging and supportive feedback. To help you do this, we suggest focusing your energy on the three skills of listening, goal setting, and giving feedback.

The first key skill, *listening*, allows us to assess another person's strengths and limitations, which builds a foundation for helping others realize their potential. Additionally, skillful listening, particularly with a focus on displaying empathy, enables effective relationship building. Coaching is about helping people get out of their comfort zones to stretch and learn. Listening to what another person says, or does not say, is a primary goal for coaching because it helps us find an appropriate balance between challenge and support. If there is too much challenge and not enough support, someone may feel overwhelmed and give up. If there is too much support and too little challenge, learning opportunities may be missed (Sanford, 1967).

In coaching, the biggest difference you can make is to encourage others to talk about their needs, interests, passions, concerns, and hopes. When listening at this level, you can focus on knowing others well enough to help them enhance their knowledge and abilities. Hearing this perspective from others helps you create opportunities and make specific suggestions for them to learn and develop. From personal experience, when Marcy coaches others, she listens intently for what they need and where they are, and then she tailors her response appropriately. Marcy has found that only after this careful listening can she know whether to offer suggestions when someone is not stretching enough or, the opposite, to offer support if the person is reaching too far.

This approach to listening connects with the second key skill of coaching: *goal setting*. Coaching works most effectively when a person identifies a direction in which to focus; goals help define this direction in the clearest way. Creating opportunities for others means helping them identify how they want to improve and seeking out different ways for them to develop. When we encourage others to set goals, we must also support them in reaching those goals. Sometimes this means challenging them, whereas other times it means supporting them when something is difficult.

Balancing challenge and support is also essential when we consider the third skill of coaching others: *giving feedback*. It is difficult to learn how to give feedback so that it can be heard and integrated. Consider the BOOST model of feedback (Giving feedback, n.d.). BOOST stands for *balanced*, *observed*, *owned*, *specific*, and *timely*. This means that feedback is best when what you say is both affirming and developmental (balanced); based on facts (observed); stated from your perspective, for example "I felt ignored when you ... " (owned); detailed (specific); and given as soon as possible (timely).

> Effective coaching involves providing the perfect mixture of encouragement and distance. Coaching does not mean providing solutions and answers, but instead providing another individual with the courage to solve his/her own problems.
>
> —*Eden B. Bunch, Texas State University graduate student, involved in graduate student affairs council and in national student affairs and academic advising associations*

For example, imagine you are part of a leadership learning community that meets weekly. One member of your group, Asher, seems to be very excited about the group, but he talks a lot during the meetings and does not leave much space for others to contribute. To provide this feedback you may say, "Asher, I am really excited that we are in this learning community together and that you have so much energy about what we are working on. During last night's meeting about the community service project we have coming up, I had a hard time sharing my ideas and perspectives. I noticed that others did as well. I feel like you have a lot of great information to share, but this leaves the rest of us little time and space to share our thoughts." This feedback meets the BOOST guidelines and can likely open up a discussion with Asher for him to respond, reflect, and perhaps even alter his behavior in future meetings. By providing Asher this feedback, you are coaching him to learn from the experience.

Find Your Approach

To develop your own coaching capacity, realize that many different models and approaches to coaching exist. A search on the Web will reveal a wide variety of strategies, models, and theories of coaching that are implemented and researched worldwide. We have found, though, that a simple model like BOOST can work quite well. Keep in mind that a genuine coaching relationship begins with the relationship itself. Key components like mutual respect, learning from each other, feedback, and setting goals are all important for coaching to be effective. Ultimately, when the relationship works, individuals, groups, and organizations benefit in the long run.

Student Voices

Effective coaching is all about challenging students to think about how the work they do influences their development as an individual as well as the community around them. It is about supporting student initiatives while making sure that no one is becoming too complacent and just working to get things done for no reason.

—*Daniel DeHollander, University of Arizona graduate student, involved in the Disney College Program alumni association, as a Greek Life graduate intern, and a student affairs outreach graduate assistant*

Coaching others involves two learners. One person is learning some material or skill, and the other person is learning the best way to motivate this person to be the best that they can be. A good coach recognizes that he or she will always be learning on the job and that each new person will present a new lesson.

—*Nathan Dills, Michigan Tech junior, involved in honors society, parish council, campus student foundation, pre-health association, and study abroad*

Effective coaching is hard to describe because everyone responds differently, but the most important things coaches can do is listen, set an example, provide some perspective, and trust the people they are coaching with responsibilities.

—*Anna-Lisa Castle, Cornell University senior, involved in an undergraduate fellowship, women of color coalition, women's resource center, water polo, and an honors society*

References

Avolio, B. J. (2005). *Leadership development in balance*. Mahwah, NJ: Lawrence Erlbaum Associates.

Giving feedback using the BOOST model. (n.d.). http://toolkit.goodpractice.com/mdt/resources/development-cycle/training-cycle-delivery/delivering-learning-and-development/giving-feedback-using-the-boost-model

Goleman, D. (2000). Leadership that gets results. *Harvard Business Review*, March–April, 78–90.

London, M. (2002). *Leadership development: Paths to self-insight and professional growth*. Mahwah, NJ: Erlbaum.

McCauley, C. D., & Van Velsor, E. (Eds.). (2003). *The Center for Creative Leadership handbook of leadership development*. San Francisco, CA: Jossey-Bass.

Sanford, N. (1967). *Where colleges fail*. San Francisco, CA: Jossey-Bass.

Reflection Questions

- Who are some people who have helped you along the way? Based on this chapter's explanation of coaching, would you consider them coaches? Why or why not?

- Have you seen coaching in your organization or workplace? If so, how have you experienced it? If not, how could coaching help?

- What do you think you do well that would make you an effective coach? What might you need to improve so you could be more effective as a coach?

- When has a close friend, coach, or mentor challenged you to go to the next level? Did they also support you as needed?

Chapter 15 Capitalizing on Difference

Benefiting from multiple perspectives. **Capitalizing on difference means recognizing that our unique identities, perspectives, and experiences are assets, not barriers. Emotionally intelligent leaders appreciate and use difference as an opportunity to create a broader perspective.**

Embracing Differences

In the late 1960s, in his first year as the men's basketball coach at Texas Western University, Don Haskins decided to break the mold of the collegiate team. He realized to have a championship-caliber team, he had to recruit players from vastly different locales. Recruiters found players in Detroit, New York, and other northern cities to play for the university. This choice was radical because each of these new recruits was African American. Remember, the timeframe for this story was the late 1960s.

> Working together strategically is only effective when there are diverse ideas incorporated to find the best solution.
> —*Courtney A. Woods, Michigan State University junior, involved in public speaking, community service, and volunteering*

In the 2006 film *Glory Road*, we see Haskins succeed in his recruiting effort and lead his team to the NCAA national championship game. Throughout the movie, we see characters learning how to play together as a team. The players, both African American and White, came to campus viewing the world based on their own assumptions, and each had those assumptions tested by being on a racially integrated team. The story shows how some students felt forced into unwanted relationships. Confrontations and conflicts abounded. And yet, they shared a common goal, which led them to find common ground.

One of the many story lines in the movie was how this diverse group of young men came together as a team. They overcame differences among themselves. The turning point in the story was when they came to accept and embrace their individual differences. They learned how to build strengths from their difference. Although the coach helped in this process, the movie shows how the students on the team stepped up to confront one another, challenge their own biases, and develop a sense of camaraderie and team by bringing their talents together.

Groups can often reach the most effective solutions when they integrate many perspectives on a single issue. In this manner, difference among people is not only a strength, but also a necessary condition for success.

—*Tiffany Burba, University of Maryland, College Park senior, involved in campus student judicial board, residence life, campus newspaper, club soccer, and a pre-law fraternity*

Difference Matters

It may sound trite, but there is great truth in the statement that the world is shrinking and we live in an interconnected, global society. If you have had the opportunity to work in the public or private sector, you may have seen this in action. One of the implications of being interconnected is that we face differences all around us, both frequently and unintentionally. More so now than ever before, we encounter people with different ideas, perspectives, nationalities, religions, abilities, talents, and so on.

Research suggests a person's values and practices, which are linked to society and culture, affect what leaders do and how they interact with others; they also affect the culture and practices of their organizations (House, Javidan, Hanges, & Dorfman,

2002). Thus, it is important to understand how our values and perspectives influence our approach to leadership. When we recognize that we might not only see the world differently or possess different skills but also have different core values, then we uncover the reason why we may struggle to find common ground or shared goals with another person. As you get involved in leadership, you also recognize how and why other people may differ in their approaches to leadership (Ayman & Korabik, 2010).

Wheel of Difference

Throughout the book, we have explored the importance of self-awareness and knowing yourself. Capitalizing on difference begins with self-awareness—understanding what makes up your own identity helps you to identify why and how you are different from others. What makes you who you are? We suggest there are four realms that comprise our identity: our core, social identities, other identities, and experiences (see Figure 15.1). Each realm exists in relation to the others within the wheel.

The wheel of difference helps define our sense of self, our relationship to others, and how we see the world in which we live. Our *core* is central to our identity; it is the essence of who we are. It is what makes each of us unique and is made up of our personality, our values, and our beliefs. The core exists in relation to the other realms. At times, the three realms support our core. At other times, our core may conflict with dimensions or elements that comprise the other realms of our identity.

The realm of *social identities* is made up of mostly innate aspects of who we are. Elements of our social identities are gender identity, race, ethnicity, sexual orientation, age, ability, and socioeconomic status. These elements are generally set at birth and reflect our social group membership (Jones & McEwen, 2000; Shriberg & Shriberg, 2011; Terrell & Lindsey, 2009). Our social identities help define who we are as well as provide us natural affinities with others. When we think about community

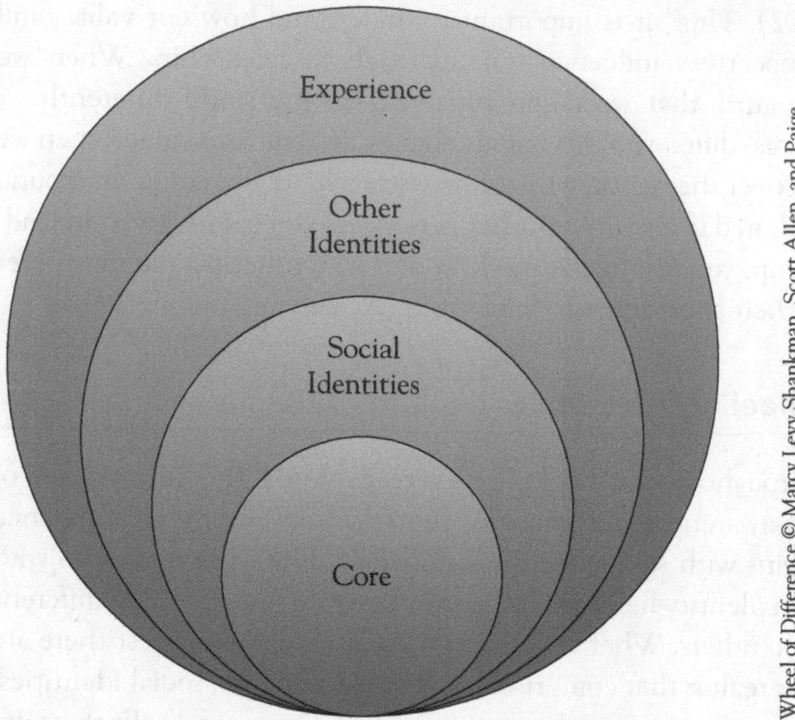

Wheel of Difference © Marcy Levy Shankman, Scott Allen, and Paige Haber-Curran.

Figure 15.1 The Wheel of Difference

or finding connections with others, often these social identities serve as anchors.

The next realm in the wheel of difference is *other identities*. These elements vary over time based on life circumstances, social and societal influences, and choices we make or that others may make for us. For example, as adults we choose our geographic location, but as children, our family status is chosen by others. Elements that make up this realm include:

marital status	geographic location
religion	nationality
income	family status
physical appearance	upbringing

> Difference is the key to a strong team. It provides a balance.
> —*Kristoffer Vo, Portland State University junior, involved in residence life*

The outermost realm, *experience*, reflects how we are also influenced by what we have done and what we are currently doing. We develop through education, acquired knowledge, work experience, employment level, field of employment, hobbies, area of study, and personal habits, which are more variable than the other components of our identity (Gardenswartz & Rowe, 1994). These elements are the most dynamic and fluctuate over time. Our choices on a daily basis affect our experience, as do the other realms and our stage in life. Our experience has both direct and indirect influence on how we know ourselves.

The wheel of difference reflects the complexity of identity. Some aspects of your wheel of difference may vary over time or because of life circumstances, while other aspects may not fluctuate at all. Awareness of our core and the elements of the other three realms help us understand who we are, why we may see the world the way we do, and how we connect or conflict with others. Understanding the elements of these circles and how they interact also helps us better accept, appreciate, and value other people and the differences they may bring to a group or situation.

Assets, Not Barriers

Seeing all the ways that we may be different can be overwhelming. Capitalizing on difference suggests that we have the potential to maximize one another's capacities on the basis of us being unique individuals. Differences, therefore, are seen as assets, not barriers. One example of this comes from more than thirty years of research and work in the Gallup Organization. Rath and Conchie (2009) found that leadership is most effective in a group or organization when members of the team possess different strengths. The premise of their model of strengths-based leadership is that the best teams are made up of people who have complementary and different strengths. According to this model, we each contribute to the team in a more significant way when our strengths differ from others on the team and when we know how to leverage these differences as assets. Thus, difference is not a problem—difference actually *makes* the difference!

> People have differing opinions. Diversity can hinder an immediate cohesive solution; however, teams that manage diverse thinking positively, often arrive at the best solutions.
>
> —*Colin Neidert, John Carroll University graduate student, works in the consumer packaged food industry*

Strengths are another way of recognizing difference. As the circles of difference suggest, difference is multifaceted and encompasses what we do, our attitudes and beliefs, our passions, our skills, our social identities, and our backgrounds. Being aware of and learning about these dimensions of differences expand our understanding of others as well as ourselves. Based on this understanding, we can learn to use differences to strengthen individuals and groups. This is where the power of capitalizing on difference really lies.

Choose the Challenge

Capitalizing on difference is a capacity that challenges each of us on a variety of levels. We may feel most comfortable by sticking with what or whom we know—focusing on our similarities. But in today's world, this choice is getting harder to make and proving to be less and less beneficial. Although difference may challenge us and lead to discomfort and conflict, it also offers untapped potential. When difference is understood and effectively leveraged, new opportunities, creative problem solving, broader understanding, and the possibility of transformative change are more likely. This is evident in many contexts across the globe, in our communities, on our campuses, in our organizations, and in ourselves.

Like leadership development, capitalizing on difference is a lifelong process. There will be situations and people that may make us uncomfortable or take us outside of our comfort zone. Think of these as opportunities to continue to develop the capacity of capitalizing on difference. By developing other EIL capacities such as emotional self-perception, empathy, authenticity, developing relationships, and building teams, we can successfully move past viewing difference as a hindrance and see it as a great opportunity.

Student Voices

We all have different strengths, weaknesses, and experiences that make us who we are. By bringing our differences together, we can look at things in ways we haven't before, we can use our strengths to help others, and we can address our own weaknesses to expand upon and improve them and become stronger—as individuals and as groups.

—*Elizabeth Vandenbil, Michigan State University sophomore, involved in residence life, student mentoring, and the honors college*

Embracing and encouraging difference fosters a certain amount of independence, pride, and confidence among people, which in turn leads to bold, collaborative, strong ideas. Without difference—without dissent—there can be no productive discussion toward the best solution to a problem.

—*Nakita VanBiene, Williams College junior, involved in women's rugby and students for educational reform*

Differences among people become a source of strength when you use those differences to create a stronger and better end result. If differences only create conflict, nothing will ever get done.

—*Patricia Fabijanczyk, The Catholic University of America senior, involved in campus programming board, international affairs, Spanish club, and Habitat for Humanity*

Differences allow things to move on from status quo. They are what drive the social change engine to improve on what is already there. Difference means never settling for what's comfortable.

—*Trent Saiget, University of San Diego sophomore, involved in student leadership advisory board, Greek life, intramurals, an honors society, and as an admission tour guide*

References

Ayman, R., & Korabik, K. (2010). Leadership: Why gender and culture matter. *American Psychologist*, *65*(3), 157–170.

Gardenswartz, L., & Rowe, A. (1994). *Diverse teams at work*. New York, NY: McGraw-Hill.

House, R., Javidan, M., Hanges, P., & Dorfman, P. (2002). Understanding cultures and implicit leadership theories across the globe: An introduction to project GLOBE. *Journal of World Business*, *37*, 3–10.

Jones, S. R., & McEwen, M. K. (2000). A conceptual model of multiple dimensions of identity. *Journal of College Student Development*, *41*(4), 405–414.

Rath, T., & Conchie, B. (2009). *Strengths-based leadership: Great leaders, teams, and why people follow*. New York, NY: Gallup Press.

Shriberg, D., & Shriberg, A. (2011). *Practicing leadership: Principles and applications*. Hoboken, NJ: Wiley.

Terrell, R. D., & Lindsey, R. B. (2009). *Culturally proficient leadership: The personal journey begins within*. Thousand Oaks, CA: Corwin Press.

Reflection Questions

- In the wheel of difference, what are the different elements of your identity that directly influence leadership? How frequently do you think about these different elements and realms?

- When you are with people who are most like you, how do you feel? What about when you are with a broad mix of people?

- As you think about the groups you are a part of, how well do you think you capitalize on difference? What could you do differently to maximize these differences so that your group becomes stronger or more effective?

- What do you identify as your strengths? What strengths might you seek from others in a group in order to help move the group forward?

Chapter 16 Developing Relationships

Building a network of trusting relationships. **Developing relationships means creating meaningful connections. Emotionally intelligent leaders encourage opportunities for relationships to grow and develop.**

It's about Relationships

> The quality of your life is the quality of your relationships.
> —*Anthony Robbins, motivational speaker*

Developing relationships is a key ingredient of emotionally intelligent leadership (EIL). As Couto and Eken suggest, (2002) "Every element of leadership implies interpersonal relationships" (p. 201). Positive relationships in groups and organizations lead to increased performance, group member commitment, positive feelings, and experiences within the group (Lencioni, 2002). Simply put, individuals, groups, and organizations are stronger, smarter, and more effective when they are rooted in and facilitate positive relationships.

Often people assume that you must be outgoing and extraverted to build relationships. This is a myth. Susan Cain (2013), author of *Quiet: The Power of Introverts in a World That Can't Stop Talking*, emphasizes the value and power that people who are introverted have in building relationships. They tend to listen well, think before speaking, and enjoy deep and meaningful conversations. Developing relationships involves much more than being talkative and socializing. At its core, this EIL capacity involves working "under the assumption that nothing important gets done alone" (Goleman, Boyatzis, & McKee, 2002, p. 51).

Regardless of whether you prefer extraversion or introversion, developing relationships entails listening well, self-awareness, and knowing how to develop rapport with others. To develop relationships means you understand the valuable role that others play in effective leadership. In addition to being a key skill for demonstrating EIL, developing relationships is an essential life skill. At the heart of this capacity is knowing you accomplish more when you engage with others and help create meaningful connections.

> It's not only what you know but who you know. The more you can network, the more relationships you build, which creates endless possibilities.
> —*Maggie Rachelle Darnell, Fort Hays State University senior, involved in the cheer squad and an honor society*

Creating Connections

You have probably heard the saying "It's not what you know, it's who you know." Although we like the intention behind this saying, we do not believe it is an either/or situation. We believe both are true—it is about what you know *and* who you know. Relationships and connections are important in personal and professional realms. EIL involves being skilled at seeking out, developing, and fostering relationships with a wide range of people.

If you think about the various relationships you have, you can see they differ based on a number of variables, including in what context you know the person, how long you have known one another, and how much time you have spent together. You may notice other obvious differences: social identities (e.g., gender, race, age), values, interests, and so forth. Additionally, different relationships serve different purposes in our lives. Think about who in your life provides you with emotional support. Who advocates for you? Who is always there to listen to you? Who challenges your thinking? Who do you go to when you need help problem solving? Is this the same person who you go to when you need help advancing an idea or completing a task?

Emotionally intelligent leaders cast a wide net and develop relationships with different types of people who have diverse strengths and perspectives. People easily come together through similarities, although it is the differences among people that can strengthen relationships, stimulate creativity, and contribute to personal growth and development (see chapter 15 on capitalizing on difference). This approach to developing relationships strengthens the leadership process.

Malcolm Gladwell (2006), author of the bestselling book *The Tipping Point*, stresses the importance of building strong networks of relationships. He identifies three types of people who add value to movements:

1. *Connectors*: People who know many different people and have the social capital to bring them together.
2. *Mavens*: People who have a great deal of knowledge and information on a particular topic or series of topics.
3. *Salesmen*: People who are skilled at influencing and persuading others.

Connectors, mavens, and salesmen serve as great examples of the different roles that people can play in the leadership process. Success is a group effort, and involving people with a wide range of skills and abilities enhances group effectiveness. As an example, consider an organization planning a large-scale event. Making sure that the executive board members have a wide range of people with different skills will help make the event successful. Ideally, some members know lots of people from different social circles, academic disciplines, and groups to spread the word (connectors); other members are inspiring and can get people excited about the event (salesmen); and members who have experience with similar events can help plan and run the event (mavens). With this team, the executive board will both create and pull off a great event.

Developing relationships goes hand in hand with the EIL capacity of authenticity. When you create connections and build relationships, it is important to do so in an authentic manner.

> To build trusting relationships, you need to be honest and open about your thoughts. Do what you say you are going to do, and hold yourself accountable for your own actions.
> —*Myder Vang, Michigan Tech junior, involved in student foundation and the society of women engineers*

Connections and relationships should be forged with good intentions, not through manipulation or deceit. EIL entails creating meaningful and mutually beneficial relationships.

Networking

Returning to the quote "It's not what you know, it's who you know," a colleague of ours once said that networking is more about *who knows you* than *who you know*. To make sure that others know you, it is important to focus on creating, building, and fostering your network. Networking is a useful strategy for beginning to develop relationships or broadening your connections with others. There is a negative connotation that can sometimes come with networking as being superficial or manipulative. We don't see networking this way. Rather, as we see it, networking is a genuine and authentic way to build relationships that can be mutually beneficial. There are a number of benefits of networking, which include:

- increasing your access to information,
- enhancing your understanding of others,
- developing meaningful relationships,
- improving your communication skills, and
- building credibility.

At Paige's first professional conference, she set a goal of prioritizing networking during the event. She wanted to feel connected to the conference and the profession, and she thought meeting people would be a great way to do so. She was feeling a little overwhelmed because she did not know many people and was new to the profession. A mentor suggested when starting a conversation with a new person, simply introduce yourself and begin by asking questions about the person because people generally like to talk about themselves. Although this may not be a strategy for everyone or for all situations, this advice helped Paige become more comfortable with networking. Today, Paige has a wide range of colleagues and friends in the profession, and she still prioritizes networking as a strategy for continuing to develop and strengthen her relationships.

> Your network is your net worth. The people you meet and have surrounding you in some ways can determine your worth as a professional. Understanding the role that people I meet can play in my future success and the importance of maintaining those relationships has produced invaluable benefits.
> —*D'Andrea Young, Texas State University graduate student, involved in a national association for student affairs, an alumni association, and as a graduate residence director*

With an increasing number of online resources available, networking expands time and place into the virtual world. Through social media and online professional platforms, there are multiple ways to connect with people across the globe. It is important to build your online presence and intentionally use social media to develop relationships with others in your field or interest areas. Although social media for some is a great tool for forming and maintaining connections, relying solely on one medium will limit the depth of your relationships. Taking the time and making the extra effort to reach out and call someone or spend face-to-face time with people makes a difference.

Fostering Relationships

Once you create a connection, you must continue to feed, foster, and nurture the relationship so that it matures and strengthens. One of the best ways to nurture relationships is to listen and be present. Learning how to focus on a conversation without being distracted by what is happening around you, notifications from

The best ways to build trusting relationships is showing people that you care, being their advocate when needed, and a willingness to listen.
—*Justin Frago, California State University, Monterey Bay sophomore, involved in the residence hall council and as an orientation leader*

your cell phone, or the to-do list festering in your mind makes people feel valued. EIL means demonstrating strong social skills, creating shared goals, and developing rapport (Goleman et al., 2002). Relationships take time to grow and strengthen, and many other EIL capacities (e.g., authenticity, flexibility, and displaying empathy) are vital to doing so.

Student Voices

When building relationships, I first seek to discover what other people value and how they like to have fun. Then, I act accordingly to honor their values and to have a good time.

—*Natalie Foster, Loyola University Chicago senior, involved in student theater, quidditch team, and serves as a housing intern*

Being genuine is the key to building trusting relationships. Putting up a front will only serve to alienate you and to create an environment of suspicion among your peers.

—*Tiffany Burba, University of Maryland–College Park senior, involved in campus student judicial board, residence life, campus newspaper, club soccer, and a pre-law fraternity*

Through networking, individuals are able to go beyond their own experiences and reach places that otherwise may not be possible.

—*Scott Willis, John Carroll University junior, involved in the student alumni association, intramural sports, and as a tour guide, orientation leader, and student athletic trainer*

Networking leads to relationships with people who have different backgrounds and much advice to offer. Never pass up an opportunity to network—you never know how you will grow as a person by meeting someone new.

—*Elizabeth Vandenbil, Michigan State University sophomore, involved in the residence hall association, the honors college, and as a mentor*

References

Cain, S. (2013). *Quiet: The power of introverts in a world that can't stop talking.* New York, NY: Broadway Books.

Couto, D., & Eken, S. (2002). *To give their gifts.* Nashville, TN: Vanderbilt University Press.

Gladwell, M. (2002). *The tipping point: How little things can make a big difference.* New York, NY: Back Bay Books.

Goleman, D., Boyatzis, R., & McKee, A. (2002). *Primal leadership: Learning to lead with emotional intelligence.* Boston, MA: Harvard Business School Press.

Lencioni, P. (2002). *The five dysfunctions of a team: A leadership fable.* San Francisco, CA: Jossey-Bass.

Reflection Questions

- How comfortable are you with meeting new people? How well do you build rapport?

- Who are the connectors, mavens, and salespeople in your organization and/or outside of your organization?

- Which relationships have influenced your development and how?

- What people or organizations will help you build your network? How might you connect with them?

- Who in your life has a strong and vibrant network? How has this benefited them?

- How would you describe you online presence? What messages does it portray? How does it support building meaningful relationships? How might it get in the way?

Chapter 17 Building Teams

Working with others to accomplish a shared purpose. **Building teams is about effectively communicating, creating a shared purpose, and clarifying roles to get results. Emotionally intelligent leaders foster group cohesion and develop a sense of "we."**

Teamwork Makes the Dream Work

When talking about teamwork in class, one of Scott's students enthusiastically said, "*Teamwork makes the dream work!*" We couldn't agree more. Building teams is a crucial skill, and effective teams facilitate good communication, create a shared purpose, clarify roles, and get results. Teams are different than groups because they require interdependence, whereby members work collaboratively, hold each other accountable, and are committed to a common purpose (Northouse, 2012). Effective teams produce results that exceed the collective capabilities of individuals. "With a group, the whole is often equal to or less than the sum of its parts; with a team, the whole is always greater" (Oakley, Felder, Brent, & Elhhajj, 2004, p. 13).

Across many industries and professions, organizations, businesses, and bosses increasingly emphasize and, in many cases, demand employees to work with others and in teams. In fact, across a number of academic disciplines, collaborative leadership was identified as the most commonly noted desired learning outcome in that major (Sharp, Komives, & Fincher, 2011). A quick Web search on the top skills sought in college graduates suggests employers across various industries are seeking the skills of teamwork, working effectively with others, effective communication, listening skills, and social intelligence. These skills can even be more desirable than technical skills required for a job.

> To effectively build a team you must have a common understanding of the end goal and the capacity to compromise.
> —*Anderson Sumarli, Cornell University senior, involved in a leadership program and an Indonesian cultural organization*

We versus Me

A key characteristic of building teams is creating a shared purpose and committing to shared goals. Vince Lombardi, National Football League coach of the Green Bay Packers during the 1960s, emphasized the importance of teamwork when he suggested the following: "Individual commitment to a group effort—that is what makes a team work, a company work, a society work, a civilization work." Whether you have played a team sport, been part of a theater crew, or been involved in any sort of group that worked well, you have experienced the strength and power of teamwork.

It is also likely that you have witnessed the challenges that ensue when teamwork is lacking. Often a team with good skills and strong teamwork can outplay a team with a few exceptional players and poor teamwork. Obviously, the best scenario is when the team is made up of exceptional players who demonstrate strong teamwork. These observations translate to group projects in class, organizations, work teams, ROTC programs, and even friendship groups and families.

Building teams from a leadership perspective means focusing on the essential building block: the individual. Individuals bring unique experiences, skills, and perspectives to a team. Teams are comprised of differentiated roles, both formal (e.g., president, marketing director, community service chair) and informal (e.g., motivator, devil's advocate, spokesperson). Being aware of and clarifying these roles is important for a group to work together effectively.

> Effective teams are built on a good work ethic, mutual respect, and a common goal.
> —*Sarah Strozeski, North Carolina State University senior, involved in university scholars, marching band, pep band, a religious organization, Habitat for Humanity, and as an ambassador*

Unfortunately, many of us are familiar with the leader who does not trust others and does everything on his or her own. This situation does not lead to long-term sustainable results, for the leader or for the team. As stated earlier, building teams means recognizing the relationships among individuals on a team as interdependent rather than independent. Prominent leadership scholar Margaret Wheatley (2002) wrote, "Relationships are all there is. Everything in the universe only exists because it is in relationship to everything else. Nothing exists in isolation. We have to stop pretending we are individuals that can go it alone" (p. 19). When seen this way, team members understand their role, value the roles and contributions of others, and work together toward a shared purpose.

It's a Process

Henry Ford, founder of Ford Motor Company, once said, "Coming together is a beginning; keeping together is progress; working together is success." Consistent with many other EIL capacities, building teams is a process, and you must continually develop and refine your capacity to build teams. Like any relationship, teams take time to develop. Tuckman (1965) describes a group's development as a team as a four-stage process:

1. *Forming*: The team comes together and people get to know each other. In this stage, the team begins to agree on goals and determines how to work together.

2. *Storming*: Team members voice differing ideas or perspectives, which can cause tension within the group. At this stage, emotions can run high, and conflicts often arise. The group must resolve how to progress through this stage to improve itself; however, sometimes groups get stuck here.
3. *Norming*: The team begins focusing on a common goal with deeper understanding and awareness. Team members agree upon new behavioral norms, and some members let go of their own ideas and personal goals to help the team function. In this stage, members become more committed to, and take responsibility for, the team and their role in the team. Interdependence is taking shape.
4. *Performing*: The team works effectively together and can tackle new goals or challenges, come to consensus, and create results.

> I think it is important to plan some sort of activity to bond and break the ice by doing something fun, getting to know each other, and gaining trust in each other before doing the task that needs to be completed together—that way you know you can rely on your team.
>
> —*Hannah Sullivan, high school sophomore from Beachwood, Ohio, involved in student council and lacrosse*

Teams experience these stages at different rates during their development. Not all teams make it to performing. And at times, teams may regress with the addition of new members or because of unresolved conflict. In these cases, the teams must work through this process again, which is not often smooth or easy.

In addition to Tuckman's stages, Patrick Lencioni (2002), author of *The Five Dysfunctions of a Team*, identifies five dysfunctions that can negatively affect a team's performance. Through examining these dysfunctions, we can identify key commitments team members can make to help build an effective team. These dysfunctions, and resulting commitments to combat these dysfunctions, follow:

Five Dysfunctions of a Team	Five Commitments for an Effective Team
1. Absence of trust	1. Opening up and building trust within the team
2. Fear of conflict	2. Engaging in respectful discourse and conflict
3. Lack of commitment	3. Committing to the team's purpose
4. Avoidance of accountability	4. Holding oneself and others accountable for their performance
5. Inattention to results	5. Focusing on collective results

Source: Adapted from Lencioni, P. (2002). *The five dysfunctions of a team: A leadership fable*. San Francisco, CA: Jossey-Bass.

Imagine a small group of students coming together around a common cause to charter a new student organization. Many different ideas are circulating within the group on the organization's purpose and events the organization may host for the coming year. With so many different ideas and perspectives, people are not on the same page and have varying levels of commitment to the organization. At this point, the organization can go one of two ways: the members can remain disjointed without a collective purpose, or they can come together and start to become a team.

The Five Dysfunctions of a Team framework provides insight into this situation. Lencioni (2002) suggests that first, and foremost, team members must be open and vulnerable with each other. "Great teams do not hold back with one another. . . . They are unafraid to air their dirty laundry. They admit their mistakes, their weaknesses, and their concerns without fear of reprisal" (p. 44). With a healthy level of trust, the team can begin to feel comfortable engaging in meaningful conversations and members can feel comfortable bringing up differing perspectives. Team

> The strength of the team is each individual member. The strength of each member is the team.
> —*Phil Jackson, former National Basketball Association coach*

members can then begin prioritizing goals for the organization. Although discourse and conflict can be difficult, they are crucial factors in building an effective team. Without this happening, team members will not come together and eventually the group falls apart. By engaging in a healthy level of conflict, team members begin to more fully commit to the purpose of the team, hold each other accountable, and work collectively to achieve team goals. This process obviously is fortified with EIL, especially with the capacities of managing conflict, developing relationships, authenticity, and citizenship.

Communication Is Key

Have you ever participated in a teambuilding or ropes course activity or worked with others to try to address a complex challenge? Paige served as a ropes course facilitator and worked with a diverse array of teams. She designed challenges that teams needed to work through, such as getting everyone to climb a wall or get through an obstacle course while blindfolded. After each and every challenge, team members consistently attributed communication (or lack of communication) as a key factor of the team's success (or failure).

Communication is an essential process for building teams. When communication is reciprocal in nature, and team members recognize that listening is just as important, if not more important, than speaking, teams become even stronger.

Consider the ways in which you communicate within a group or team. Do you voice your ideas and opinions when it's important to do so? Do you build on and add to others' ideas? Do you take time to listen, and we mean *really listen*, to what others are saying? Are you comfortable with silence? Are you aware of what messages your nonverbal cues may be communicating to the group? We cannot stress enough the significant role communication plays in building teams *and* emotionally intelligent leadership.

Student Voices

Establishing clear objectives and identifying the roles each member will play is essential to team cohesion. Without it, there is no way to stay on the same page.

—*Ty McTigue, John Carroll University senior, involved in orientation, tutoring, and Greek life*

A strong team consists of individuals from various backgrounds, experiences, and values, yet who are like-minded in the sense that they share a common goal. I particularly enjoy taking leadership and personality inventories such as the Myers-Briggs to see what my team members are like and how we can complement each other's strengths and weaknesses.

—*Brenda Shah, University of Maryland, College Park sophomore, involved in a peer leadership council, the residence hall association, a pre-health fraternity, and as a resident assistant and honors college ambassador*

To build a strong team you have to surround yourself with the best people you can. The most successful people in the world are not necessarily the smartest—they were just able to bring together brilliant people to work for a common goal.

—*Michael Shea, East Carolina University sophomore, involved in student conduct, a leadership organization, and as a tutor*

Everyone on the team has an asset to contribute for the betterment of the team. Without realizing everyone's capabilities, a team cannot function as a cohesive group.

—*David Tassone, Loyola Marymount University sophomore, involved in student government and a religious organization, and as a resident advisor and track coach*

References

Lencioni, P. (2002). *The five dysfunctions of a team: A leadership fable*. San Francisco, CA: Jossey-Bass.

Northouse, P. G. (2012). *Leadership: Theory and practice* (6th ed.). Thousand Oaks, CA: Sage.

Oakley, B., Felder, R., Brent, R., & Elhhajj, I. (2004). Turning student groups into effective teams. *Journal of Student-Centered Learning*, *2*(1), 9–34.

Sharp, M. D., Komives, S. R., & Fincher, J. (2011). Learning outcomes in academic disciplines: Identifying common ground. *Journal of Student Affairs Research and Practice*, *48*(4), 481–504.

Tuckman, B. (1965). Developmental sequence in small groups. *Psychological Bulletin*, *63*(6), 384–399.

Wheatley, M. (2002). *Turning to one another: Simple conversations to restore hope to the future*. San Francisco, CA: Berrett-Koehler.

Reflection Questions

- What has been your best team experience? What about the team made it great?

- How easily do you build trust in other people?

- How comfortable are you with opening up and being vulnerable in a group?

- Which of the five dysfunctions have you experienced in a group setting? How did the dysfunctions affect the team?

- What communication strategies do you use effectively in a group? Which might you overuse? Underuse?

Chapter 18 Demonstrating Citizenship

Fulfilling responsibilities to the group. **Citizenship is about being actively engaged and following through on your commitments. Emotionally intelligent leaders meet their ethical and moral obligations for the benefit of others and the larger purpose.**

A key aspect of being part of any group or community is recognizing and fulfilling the responsibilities to which you have committed. Often people think of citizenship as associated with being a citizen of a country; however, in the context of emotionally intelligent leadership (EIL), citizenship involves being an active, contributing, and responsible member of a group or community. We each belong to many different groups and communities, such as colleges or universities, student organizations, community groups, places of worship, workplaces, cities or towns, and so on. Demonstrating citizenship is essential for EIL because it differentiates us from inactive or noncontributing members of a group. Thus, demonstrating citizenship is vital for a group, organization, cause, or community to thrive.

> It is not always the same thing to be a good [person] and a good citizen.
>
> —*Aristotle, Greek philosopher*

We Are Part of a Larger Whole

Demonstrating citizenship involves recognizing that you are part of something bigger than yourself. Inherent in this capacity is acknowledging that at times you must set aside your personal interests for the betterment of the larger group. Of course, this commitment (like all the EIL capacities) can be taken to an unhealthy extreme. In general, citizenship involves living by a set of standards that means you will, when appropriate and needed, put others ahead of yourself. Practicing citizenship involves

- active engagement in accordance with the values of the group;
- fulfilling responsibilities to the group and its members; and
- meeting the ethical and moral obligations inherent in the values of the community.

How an individual lives each of these statements depends, in large measure, on what the organization, group, or community expects of its members. For the purposes of illustration, consider the following examples we draw from our experiences of working with students:

- *Greek organization*: Living your ritual, following through on formal and informal commitments (e.g., giving your time, paying your dues), supporting chapter members, participating in philanthropic events, upholding the standards of your organization, and being active as an alumnus
- *Internship*: Arriving on time, asking for work when you are finished with your current project load, being known as a team player, and vocalizing your enthusiasm for and showing a commitment to the purpose or vision of the organization
- *Athletic team*: Arriving to practice and games on time, responding to the coach's instructions, challenging and supporting teammates, engaging in fair play, modeling team values, and demonstrating a strong commitment to fellow team members
- *Resident assistant/advisor*: Being available to your residents, building a sense of community within the residence hall, working collaboratively with your fellow resident assistants, fulfilling your formal responsibilities, and having a commitment to the larger residential life organization
- *Student government*: Conducting work with your constituents' interests in mind, modeling ethical behavior, supporting the

values of the institution, serving as an ambassador to administrators, setting policy, and following through on commitments

- *Tour guide/Orientation leader*: Staying current on campus issues, maintaining a positive attitude when meeting prospective students and families, supporting the values of the institution, providing trustworthy information, and serving as a good role model
- *In the classroom*: Going to class, being prepared, following through on your commitments to others in group projects, actively participating in discussion, and doing your own best work (e.g., avoiding cheating and plagiarism)

In each of these examples, demonstrating citizenship involves moving beyond self-interest to prioritize the group or community. Although these examples are focused on the collegiate experience, you likely can identify other contexts or points in your life when you have experienced leadership as being about "we," not just "me."

We All Play a Part in the Leadership Equation

> Active group members not only do what is expected of them, but are proactive and willing to fill in the gaps.
> —*Cicely Shannon, University of Arkansas junior, involved in student government, pre-law society, service organization, and an honors society*

Demonstrating citizenship is a key aspect of effective leadership, yet it runs counter to a common sentiment within many societies that leaders lead and followers follow. This bias, the idea that leadership is a solo act, is all around us. In essence, people who are not "the leader" are often left out of a discussion on leadership, even though the role of group members is vital in enacting leadership. Kelley (1995) makes this point by suggesting, "Organizations stand or fall partly on the basis of how well their leaders lead, but partly also on the basis of how well their followers follow" (p. 193). Kelley recognized the important role that everyone plays in an organization, no matter what role is held. Engaged group members are committed to the organization and its purpose; work hard and have high standards of performance; act in line with the values and mission of the organization; and are credible and dependable.

> People must feel valued in the group. In order to encourage commitment, I strongly believe that recognition for one's accomplishments is necessary.
>
> —*Brenda Shah, University of Maryland sophomore, involved in a peer leadership council, the residence hall association, a pre-health fraternity, and as a resident assistant and honors college ambassador*

Enabling Group Citizenship

As a member of a group or organization, you can play an important role in encouraging and enabling citizenship in others. Some may say this is the responsibility of the people who hold leadership positions. We think this reflects a narrow, positional definition of leadership. EIL means that enabling group citizenship is everyone's responsibility in a group or organization. We have seen the success of groups and organizations when everyone shares responsibility for the group. Unfortunately, it is common for students in leadership positions to have a hard time allowing other people in the organization to take on responsibilities. Some students have had experiences with group members in the past who did not follow through on commitments or fulfill responsibilities, which can lead them to take on the attitude of "I will just do it all myself."

Taking everything on yourself, however, is not sustainable for you or the organization. It is important to examine your organization to ensure that members have multiple ways to be engaged, involved, and committed. Is everyone aware of the mission and values of the organization? Does everyone know what it means to act in line with the mission and values? Are expectations set for what it means to be an active member in the organization? Do people feel appreciated and recognized for their contributions? Are there ways for members to have a voice?

> To get others more involved, I specifically reach out to each individual and figure out what's holding them back from the group or organization so I am able to point out things I know they would like to draw them in.
> —*Saige Eitman, high school junior in Beachwood, Ohio, involved in theater, youth group, and the social action club*

Demonstrating citizenship involves creating the space for others to actively participate and have a say in what happens. It also encompasses recognizing that you are part of something bigger than yourself. Capitalizing on the other EIL capacities (e.g., taking initiative, building teams, inspiring others) can help you engage in active citizenship as well as help encourage and enable others to play an active role in the organization.

Student Voices

When the entire group is contributing, it provides a cohesive environment for producing the best outcome. Everyone is engaged and the final product is something of which everyone can be proud.

—*Aime Szymanski, John Carroll University senior, involved in Greek life, honor societies, and club lacrosse*

An active member goes beyond the minimum attendance of meetings and functions to truly improve the group. She asks, "What mark will I make on this group? How can my membership be beneficial?"

—*Madeline Mariana Schulz, Texas A&M University sophomore, involved in the traditions council and as a counselor for an extended orientation program*

Active citizenship involves contributing ideas and helping out where needed, but it does not mean you follow the leader blindly. Instead, you challenge the leader when you think he or she is wrong because you are both invested in achieving the same goal, and you will do anything you can to achieve that goal.

—*Michael Shea, East Carolina University sophomore, involved in student conduct, a leadership organization, and as a tutor*

Giving group members tasks and responsibilities early and trusting them to complete those tasks is the key to keeping them engaged and committed.

—*TJ Fisher, Rollins College senior, involved in an honor society, Greek life, an allies program, and as a tour guide*

Reference

Kelley, R. E. (1995). In praise of followers. In J. T. Wren (Ed.), *The leader's companion* (pp. 193–204). New York, NY: Free Press.

Reflection Questions

- What does it mean to be a good citizen in your organization? On your campus? In the classroom?

- What happens when an individual does not model good citizenship? What can this do to the organization?

- How can you enable citizenship in others?

- When have you struggled to demonstrate citizenship?

- How are you personally responsible for others? What are you doing differently when this is your priority?

Chapter 19 Managing Conflict

Identifying and resolving conflict. **Managing conflict is about working through differences to facilitate the group process. Emotionally intelligent leaders skillfully and confidently address conflicts to find the best solution.**

This capacity acknowledges that conflict is a part of leadership, and, when managed effectively, can foster better results. Conflict comes in many different shapes and forms. At times conflict is overt and may involve anger, raised voices, or high levels of frustration. Other times conflict is below the surface and shows itself in less obvious ways (e.g., cliques, side conversations, and apathy). When conflict is skillfully and confidently addressed, disputes and struggles are resolved, groups become stronger, individuals become more invested in the group's process, and better solutions are identified. Regardless of context (e.g., high school, college, workplace), conflict exists.

> Knowing the difference between constructive and destructive conflict is crucial for effective leadership. Though two parties can have differing opinions, approaching a conflict situation with open minds can lead to a better solution than either could alone.
>
> *—Brian Lackey, University of Texas School of Public Health graduate student, involved in a public health student association and community service*

Harnessing the potential energy inherent in conflict is a wonderful skill. Emotionally intelligent leadership (EIL) approaches conflict as a potential source of creativity and feedback. In many cases, working with or through conflict yields an increased level of ownership for everyone involved. We agree with Couto and Eken (2002), who suggest, "However much our leaders enjoy or dislike conflict, they recognize its inevitability and its primary role in clarifying values" (p. 209). Because conflict is an inherent part of leadership, we explore two key arenas: sources of conflict and approaches to managing conflict.

Sources of Conflict

Conflict arises for many different reasons. In formal and informal groups as well as organizations, eight common causes of conflict have been identified (Bell, 2002; Hart, 2000).

1. *Conflicting needs*: When conflicting needs emerge, the issue generally relates to competition for limited resources (e.g., money, attention, supplies). Power struggles often result from this source of conflict.
2. *Conflicting styles*: Based on personality differences or work styles, people often complain or struggle with one another. When someone says, "I just can't work with that person," it is usually a conflict in styles.
3. *Conflicting perceptions*: We each have our own experiences and perspectives, and these affect how we view the world, how we understand what happens to us, and even how we hear what others say. What one person hears as a joke can be offensive to another.
4. *Conflicting goals*: Although the overall mission and purpose may be the same, individual goals and benchmarks for success can vary dramatically. Likewise, people may have different viewpoints on priorities or even objectives related to goals.
5. *Conflicting pressures*: Because of different roles and responsibilities in groups and organizations, each of us experiences differing levels of pressure. An impending deadline for the leader of a program will be felt more intensely than individual members of the team.

6. *Conflicting roles*: Whether the group is formal and informal, no two individuals play the same role. This source of conflict may result from conflicting needs and goals.
7. *Conflicting values*: Similar to conflicting styles, conflict can result from a difference of values. If our personal values conflict with another's, we can experience struggles over what is right or the correct course of action.
8. *Inconsistent policies*: In formal and informal groups, there are accepted rules of behavior. Some of these are written, while others are unwritten. Regardless, if they are not predictable, either because they are frequently changed or inconsistently applied, issues emerge and conflict results.

> Conflict is like a pot of water that is left too long to boil. If stirred and taken off the heat (by using healthy conflict resolution techniques), a little hot water can lead to healthy growth and discussion. If ignored, sooner or later it will bubble up and spill over, which takes a lot more effort and time to clean up.
>
> —*Sophie Foxman, high school senior from Toronto, Ontario, involved in yearbook and a regional youth group*

When we diagnose the source of conflict, we take the first step to resolve or manage the conflict effectively (Whetten & Cameron, 2010). Unfortunately, it isn't always so easy to do this because multiple sources of conflict can be going on at the same time. Perhaps you have seen this in your own organization. Scott is reminded of several disagreements in his fraternity as the men struggled through changes that needed to occur in their new member education program. There were conflicting values (hazing is fine versus hazing is wrong), conflicting pressures (leaders being held accountable for the actions of individual members), conflicting perceptions (what constitutes hazing), and even conflicting goals (becoming the best versus status quo). Needless to say, Scott was ill equipped to navigate the many sources of conflict surrounding the issue, and although progress was made, a number of relationships were damaged in the process.

Work through Conflict

To address the different sources of conflict, consider the following approaches to managing conflict (Thomas & Kilmann, 2007). Each of these approaches is appropriate for some situations, but there is not one single approach that works best all the time. As you read through the descriptions, think about what you tend to do most often when you are trying to manage conflict. Likewise, think about what situations might be best for each approach.

- *Competing*: You are assertive and stand up for what you believe. You know how to defend your position and will do so to get your way. The downside of this approach is that others may feel alienated, bullied, or left out.
- *Compromising*: You give a little to get a little. This means you look to find the best solution for all as quickly and easily as possible. The downside of this approach is that no one is entirely happy and problems may linger.
- *Collaborating*: You strike a balance between being assertive and being cooperative. You attempt to create the "win-win" in the situation. The time and energy that is spent managing the conflict leads to an outcome that benefits all parties, without any feeling of loss or compromise. The downside of this approach is the additional time this could take.
- *Avoiding*: You are willing to give in to the situation or give up before a conflict starts. This may mean you postpone dealing with the issue or you simply withdraw from any conversation. The downside of this approach is that issues fester and are not resolved.
- *Accommodating*: You sacrifice what you want to help the situation get resolved. You put the other person's needs ahead of your own and work to find a solution to satisfy that person more than yourself. The downside of this approach is that you put the

others' needs in front of your own and as a result may become disinvested in the situation.

In addition to knowing yourself well and your own preferences for managing conflict effectively, it is important to be aware of how other people with whom you work tend to handle conflict. Everyone does so in different ways, and how people manage conflict varies across cultures (Tjosvold & Su Fang, 2004). It is important that you are aware of your default approach, its benefits and drawbacks. For example, if your default is avoiding, can you use a competing approach if need be? Likewise, do you know when it is better to just let it go (avoid) instead of competing for your way? Learning how to intentionally *choose* an approach to handling conflict based on the situation will make a difference in your leadership.

> By understanding the issue, having open discussion with the conflicting parties, and taking positive steps to move forward, one can effectively handle any conflict.
> —*Jonathan Martinez, Texas A&M University junior, involved in an extended orientation program, traditions council, and leadership organizations*

Returning to Scott's story, upon reflection he realized his default approach was competing when it came to change in his organization. He took a hard stand and by doing so, created little space for others with differing opinions. Although he was "right" (hazing is not appropriate), he may have chosen other approaches such as collaboration or compromise to seek other possible solutions. In the long run, there may have been greater buy-in and solutions that endured. He also may have maintained relationships that were damaged because of the issue.

Maintaining Harmony

A final point is that to resolve conflict effectively, you need to think about yourself, others who are involved, and the situation. Other EIL capacities can help you do this. When managing conflict, people need to feel that you care about them. Displaying empathy and developing relationships while capitalizing on difference help to achieve some sense of harmony in the midst of conflict. To do this, you must have both emotional self-perception and demonstrate emotional self-control as you create space for others to share their perspectives in the conversation. You bear responsibility to ensure that your voice is heard as well as the voices of others. If others do not feel their voices matter, conversations go underground and bigger problems may emerge.

Student Voices

Effectively handling conflict requires discovery of all underlying assumptions of both sides, and then clearly defining the issue. In 90 percent of the cases, conflict happens just because of different assumptions.

—*Volodymyr Nedoshytko, York University junior, involved as a trainer for an internship*

Handling conflict can be very difficult; however, if I understand the group of people I am working with, I can correlate my strategies accordingly. One of the main strategies I feel is very important is confrontation and understanding the source of the conflict, then acting in a coherent, respectable manner in order to solve it.

—*Zabebah Mohamed, College of Staten Island - CUNY graduate student, involved in a leadership program*

People are more willing to listen if they feel that they have been heard. You can then, as a group, discover the problem and the best solution.

—*Kacie Nice, Purdue University senior, involved in residence life, student newspaper, and student government*

It is important to be calm when handling conflict. Your own agenda should not be pushed, but rather an agenda of compromise and resolution.

—*Alex Myers, John Carroll University junior, involved in a pre-health society, intramural sports, and as teaching assistant, research assistant, and tour guide*

References

Bell, A. (2002). *Six ways to resolve workplace conflicts*. McLaren School of Business, University of San Francisco. www.usfca.edu/fac-staff/bell/article15.html

Couto, D., & Eken, S. (2002). *To give their gifts: Health, community and democracy*. Nashville, TN: Vanderbilt University Press.

Hart, B. (2000). *Conflict in the workplace*. Behavioral Consultants, P. C. www.excelatlife.com/articles/conflict_at_work.htm

Thomas, K. W., & Kilmann, R. H. (2007). *Thomas-Kilmann Conflict Mode Instrument*. Mountain View, CA: CPP, Inc.

Tjosvold, D., & Fang, S. S. (2004). Cooperative conflict management as a basis for training students in China. *Theory into Practice*, 43(1), 80–86.

Whetten, D. A., & Cameron, K. S. (2010). *Developing management skills* (8th ed.). Upper Saddle River, NJ: Pearson Prentice Hall.

Reflection Questions

- What are your preferred ways of handling conflict? What are the benefits and drawbacks of these defaults?

- What approaches to managing conflict do you see in groups around you? How effectively do you see conflict managed?

- In recognizing the many sources of conflict, what preventative and proactive actions can you take to avoid unnecessary conflict?

- Which sources of conflict do you navigate on a daily basis?

- Which sources of conflict are the most difficult for you to address?

- In the heat of the moment, are you skilled at intentionally choosing an appropriate style of conflict? Why is this skill so difficult to master?

Chapter 20 Facilitating Change

Working toward new directions. **Facilitating change is about advancing ideas and initiatives through innovation and creativity. Emotionally intelligent leaders seek to improve on the status quo and mobilize others toward a better future.**

The Different Faces of Change

Leadership is about change: seeking to improve others, our organizations, our communities, and the world in which we live. As a capacity of emotionally intelligent leadership (EIL), facilitating change means active engagement in creating change and working with others to make that happen. According to leadership scholar James MacGregor Burns (1978), "Leadership brings about real change that leaders intend" (p. 414). This is a simple, but not simplistic, statement. What does real change mean? How does a leader intend change? How does leadership bring about change?

Facilitating change takes many forms, depending heavily on the person and the situation. The source of inspiration or motivation for change may be internal or external, emotional or intellectual, based on facts or based on beliefs. A desired change may benefit one person, an organization, or an entire community. Some people act because of an injustice they experience. Others bring people together to create change because they are looking for ways to do something better or differently. Still others mobilize resources to make change happen because of external pressures requiring a community or an organization to adapt. Regardless of the circumstances, facilitating change requires a core set of skills, attitudes, and sensitivities. Also important is recognizing the different roles you can play in making change happen, especially because you cannot do it alone.

Change Is at the Core of Leadership

In *The Leadership Challenge*, James Kouzes and Barry Posner (2012) introduce the concept of challenging the process. John Kotter (1996) promotes an eight-stage process of initiating change, and James O'Toole (1995) advocates for a values-based model for leading change. Gill Robinson Hickman (2010) authored a book about how to lead change in multiple contexts. Susan Komives and Wendy Wagner (2009) emphasize positive social change as the overall goal of the social change model of leadership. All of these authors share one common belief: change is a core tenant of leadership.

Facilitating change involves demonstrating innovative thinking, seeking opportunities to improve upon the status quo, and focusing on the future. This requires embracing creative problem solving and risk taking; it also requires courage. In the face of distractions, a desire for normalcy, and resistance, facilitating change means we have to be fully engaged, focused, and prepared for the challenges of change (Lundin, 2009). When you talk with people who have started an organization from scratch or initiated even a small scale change effort, they will attest to how exhausting (and exhilarating) it is. "People change what they do ... because they are shown a truth that influences their feelings" (Kotter & Cohen, 2002, p. 1). Thus, facilitating change requires the whole self—all that you do, feel, think, and believe.

Change Is Demanding

One widespread myth about facilitating change is that all you need is a great idea, and people will buy in and follow you. In reality, facilitating change requires more than having the idea. To bring change about, you "recognize the need for change and remove barriers, challenge the status quo … enlist others" to assist in making change happen (Goleman, 2011, p. 193). Thus, you must work in concert with others in the context of a situation, which brings together all of the facets of EIL. Consciousness of self, consciousness of others, and consciousness of context are essential and interconnected when facilitating change.

> In order to create change, you need to be flexible, confident, and think outside of the box to come up with new and exciting ideas.
> —*Brittany Anne Brown, University of Maryland, College Park senior, involved in residence life*

Of course, doing this work is not easy. Being successful in this pursuit requires critical thinking, self-awareness, the ability to develop relationships, and resilience. In terms of EIL, facilitating change works when we assess the environment, build teams, and demonstrate initiative, optimism, emotional self-perception, and emotional self-control. For example, when Marcy was in college, she started a community safety initiative because of a few somewhat frightening events that took place on campus and in the community. Starting a campus-wide program meant she spent time working closely with other individuals and organizations to raise awareness as well as funding. The initiative took much longer than expected, and she faced any number of roadblocks, but because of those with whom she collaborated, she kept going. In the end, the program took almost a full year to get started, but the time was well spent because the program continued for many years thereafter.

We must be in tune with our own capacities and display empathy when working with others, all while assessing the conditions for change (Hickman, 2010). Marcy had to identify with potential collaborators so that she could engage them meaningfully in the project. Having a broad perspective (consciousness of context) is essential when considering a change, and not having a broad enough perspective hinders both the process and the results. As hard as it may be to seek new opportunities, we know from research that when leaders stop looking for new opportunities, success and effectiveness diminish (Collins, 2001). This is just one of the many reasons why facilitating change is difficult work.

Roles of Change Agents

To meet the demands of facilitating change, we each have potential roles to play. One way to think about this role is to imagine being a change agent—a person who makes change happen. The following prompts can help you consider your potential to be a change agent:

- *Are you a catalyst?* This person identifies a new idea or direction and serves as the champion for it (Cawsey & Deszca, 2007). Being a catalyst requires creativity, energy, future-focus, and a clear sense of purpose.
- *Are you an implementer?* This person brings new ideas to fruition. Being an implementer requires a commitment to action as well as the skills and persistence to design and implement a plan while rallying support and reducing resistance (Cawsey & Deszca, 2007).
- *Are you a facilitator?* This person excels at mobilizing people and resources. Based on the strength of relationships, having a systems perspective (e.g., seeing the big picture), and having high levels of self-awareness, facilitators use "their interpersonal skills to work with teams or groups" (Cawsey & Deszca, 2007, p. 8).

> If you want something changed, be that change, be the catalyst. Don't wait around for someone to take up the reins for you.
> —*Alicia Ann Bingen, University of Wisconsin, Madison junior, involved in campus leadership programs*

As you can see in the description of the three roles, various other EIL capacities go hand in hand with being a change agent. Building teams and developing relationships are critical. Taking initiative and displaying optimism are equally important. Regardless of the role(s) you may play, keep in mind the ways in which other EIL capacities support and contribute to your effective fulfillment of these roles.

Timing Is Key

Another factor that affects our ability to lead change is timing. For change to be meaningful and effective, timing is key. Unfortunately, there is no scientific formula for determining when the time is right. Thinking through your rationale and motivation for change can help inform the timing. Further, it is important to examine the larger context, identify key external forces that might influence your efforts, and assess the climate of the group of people directly affected by the change (all relating to the EIL facet of consciousness of context). Before you implement change, consider questions such as:

- Who is likely to be influenced by this change, and what needs to be done to help prepare and support them through the transition?
- Will people be available to help make the change happen?
- When will people most likely be receptive to this change?
- Where will you experience resistance? How will you respond to the resistance?
- What resources do you need to make the change happen? How will you get them?
- What other factors in the external environment can influence (either as an opportunity or threat) this change?
- Should the change take place all at once, or in steps or stages?

It is likely that when facilitating change, you will face resistance. Realize that resistance is not inherently bad. Sometimes the resistance you face may cause you to reassess your strategy and develop a new, and often better or more innovative, approach. Other times, you may find that your support is not as strong as you expected. This pause in the process allows you to work differently to assess your group or develop relationships further so that more people will become involved. Reframing resistance as a contribution to the process of change is a powerful choice that emotionally intelligent leaders make (Maurer, 2010).

The Choice Is Yours

Facilitating change is easy for some people and difficult for others. Does leading change excite or scare you? Are you looking for the possibilities of what is next, or are you content with what is? How you answer these questions directly reflects your inclination toward change. Because change is all around us, the choice is yours. Which side of change do you want to be on: making it happen or waiting for it to happen to you?

Student Voices

Positive change can be brought about by anyone who has the passion and vision to succeed, the willingness to fail and try again, and the openness and capacity to recognize leadership is defined by followers.

—*Nakita VanBiene, Williams College junior, involved in women's rugby and students for educational reform*

A change agent is someone who sets a clear vision and takes persistent steps toward achieving it. He or she is someone people can look to for motivation and who leads by example.

—*Patricia Fabijanczyk, The Catholic University of America senior, involved in campus programming board, international affairs, Spanish club, and Habitat for Humanity*

Persistence and confidence are two essential elements a leader needs if they hope to make positive and lasting change.

—*Marc Jeremy Cohen, University at Albany, State University of New York sophomore, involved in student government, a law fraternity, and as a student delegate to the university faculty senate*

References

Burns, J. M. (1978). *Leadership*. New York, NY: Harper & Row.

Cawsey, T., & Deszca, G. (2007). *Toolkit for organizational change*. Thousand Oaks, CA: Sage.

Collins, J. (2001). *Good to great: Why some companies make the leap ... and others don't*. New York, NY: Harper Business.

Goleman, D. (2011). *Working with emotional intelligence*. New York, NY: Random House.

Hickman, G. R. (2010). *Leading change in multiple contexts: Concepts and practices in organizational, community, political, social, and global change settings*. Thousand Oaks, CA: Sage.

Komives, S. R., & Wagner, W. (2009). *Leadership for a better world: Understanding the social change model of leadership development*. San Francisco, CA: Jossey-Bass.

Kotter, J. P. (1996). *Leading change*. Boston, MA: Harvard Business School Press.

Kotter, J., & Cohen, D. S. (2002). *The heart of change*. Cambridge, MA: Harvard Business Review.

Kouzes, J. M., & Posner, B. Z. (2012). *The leadership challenge* (5th ed.). San Francisco, CA: Jossey-Bass.

Lundin, S. C. (2009). *Cats: The nine lives of innovation*. New York, NY: McGraw-Hill.

Maurer, R. (2010). *Beyond the walls of resistance: Why 70% of all changes still fail—and what you can do about it*. Austin, TX: Bard Press.

O'Toole, J. (1995). *Leading change: The argument for values-based leadership*. San Francisco, CA: Jossey-Bass.

Reflection Questions

- It is important to consider your own reactions to change. What is your gut reaction to change? What does this mean for you if you want to initiate change?

- If you could have ______ any way you would like it to be, what would it look like? Fill in the blank with an area for change—a familiar context, setting, relationship, or a cause or an issue about which you are passionate. Once you've filled in the blank, think about what change you would want to see.

- Referring to the previous question, think through how you can begin to make the changes happen. What are some important first steps? Who can help? When is the right time to initiate that change process?

- What type of change agent are you? What situations may call for a different way of facilitating change?

Part Three: Consciousness of Context

Chapter 21 Consciousness of Context

Demonstrating emotionally intelligent leadership involves awareness of the setting and situation. Consciousness of context is about paying attention to how environmental factors and internal group dynamics affect the process of leadership.

Setting + Situation = Context

The context is the environment in which leaders and followers work and comprises both the setting and the situation (Fiedler, 1972). The *setting* most often refers to the environment and structure of the group or organization, for example, a business, a college sports team, the floor of a residence hall, or any formal or informal organization or group. The *situation* is more dynamic. It includes the many different forces of a particular time and place, including but not limited to individual personalities, politics, power relationships, societal trends, and tensions or challenges that emerge within the setting.

By definition, then, context changes constantly. Each new setting or situation requires people to think actively about what is needed, understood, and expected. This means that consciousness of context requires different sets of knowledge, skills, and abilities based on your understanding of the setting and situation. Here are some examples:

- The Tea Party did not exist prior to President Barack Obama's presidency. In fact, it was founded *after* he was elected. What caused the formation of this group?
- Smart phones were once just for savvy and fast-tracked business leaders. What has changed so that even a fourth-grader has one?

- Fraternities and sororities have seen an increase in reported risk management incidents. What contextual factors have affected this reality?
- LGBTQI organizations did not exist on college campuses fifty years ago. What has changed?
- Today, many residence halls are being built with single rooms. Why are roommates no longer desirable?
- It used to be that Microsoft could not fail, but when was the last time you saw someone with a Zune?
- Many students are now balancing work along with classes. How does this affect their relationship to being involved on campus?

> Context is the situation we are placed in—the people, the resources, and the problems that surround us.
> —*Cody Rutledge, University of Illinois at Chicago graduate student, involved in the student-run free clinic*

The context for leadership provides many challenges and opportunities; however, without being conscious of the context, much is lost. What happens in the environment where leadership occurs is a fundamental influence in fostering or threatening your leadership. What contextual factors supported Angela Merkel's second election as chancellor of Germany? What was happening in India when Mahatma Gandhi demonstrated nonviolent civil disobedience? Why was Steve Jobs fired in 1985 but rehired by Apple in 1997? Contextual factors significantly affect our current reality and will continue to do so. Emotionally intelligent leaders must be attuned to this reality to remain relevant.

What Works Now ...

Think about a soccer team for a moment. You have the formal leader (the coach), the followers (team members), and the context (field conditions, weather, time of day, country, level of competition). The coach may use a certain leadership style one year and experience great success given who is on the team, how they respond to her, and the quality of play in the league. However, the following season, many of the factors change. As such, the coach will likely need to change her motivational style, the workouts and practice, and her approach to bringing out the best in the team to remain successful. If the coach is unable to understand and adapt to the needs of each player and the overall context, she will not be effective or successful in achieving the desired outcomes.

A number of assumptions are embedded in this scenario. Many people assume that what has worked well in the past will work again in the future. They do not take the time or pay attention to the specific needs, interests, or abilities of their group members. Most often, they do not stop to think about the setting and situation—what is different this year from last? They may falsely assume that when something is not working, the reason is the followers—they did not understand, they did not do what was asked, and so forth. Consciousness of context reminds us that other forces are at play. Alignment of action and organizational culture is essential. In a business setting, for example, Liden and Antonakis (2009) found that when leaders and followers work together and demonstrate behaviors that correspond with the values of the team or workgroup, they are viewed as more effective.

A Work-Based Scenario

Consider another example. Miranda works in the digital communications industry and has a history of selling more product than her peers. She is rapidly promoted to manager. Her store is located in a popular mall in an upper-middle-class suburb with a customer base interested in obtaining the newest and best technology as soon as it is available. Miranda loves the product, is respected by her team, and works hard to get the best deal for her customers. In essence, she has earned the respect of her team and higher-level management. Her knowledge, skills, and abilities (self) mesh well with the store environment (context) and her team (others).

Now imagine that Miranda gets transferred to a low-performing store in an economically challenged suburb of the same city. She inherits a team that consistently underperforms and sales goals have not been met in more than six months. (You can probably see where this is going.) Miranda still needs to manage a team and bring her knowledge, skills, and abilities to the workplace, but the change in store location and sales team will likely require her to use different skills and behaviors. In this new context, she will need to learn the needs of her new client base. Likewise, there may be different sales goals, metrics, and markers for success. In this new setting, she will need to learn the cultural norms and values of the community and the store, trends, employee characteristics, and expectations. These are all factors of the context that will affect Miranda's effectiveness as a leader.

> True leadership is demonstrated when situations that seem daunting are overcome with boldness, hope, and perseverance.
> —*Monica Hernandez, University of Texas School of Public Health graduate student, involved in a student organization for global health and a fellowship program in public policy*

In essence, Miranda's success will be determined in many ways by her ability to adjust to this new context. If she is not aware of the need to adapt and is not intentionally approaching this situation with these concepts at the forefront of her mind, she will likely be unsuccessful in meeting the challenges. She must consciously learn about her new setting, assess the situation, and determine what knowledge, skills, and abilities she needs to demonstrate so that she can be successful.

Context Is Key

EIL involves inspiring and meeting the needs of a group or community in a dynamic and changing world. Consciousness of context is pivotal in this process.

Think of a time when you experienced great success in leadership. Now think of a time when you failed. In all likelihood little about you changed; however, your context probably did.

Being aware of context is vitally important to EIL. Consciousness of context requires the ability to look within your organization as well as outside of it to understand what may be influencing your organization or your role, what opportunities may exist, and what challenges may arise. Thus, the two consciousness of context capacities are:

1. Analyzing the group
2. Assessing the environment

Student Voices

Every different situation needs a unique leadership approach depending on those involved and the abilities of the leader.

—*Zachary Folk, University of Missouri junior, involved in residence life, student senate, Greek Life, and an intensive language program in China*

Factors affecting a leader can originate from friends and family to school and work to the past and the present. It's important to know when an outside force is causing stress and to make sure it doesn't control your actions in the present.

—*Kevin Golla, University of North Dakota senior, involved in the campus wellness center*

Being involved in a leadership position with my fraternity really meant I had to be aware of the different perspectives my brothers brought with them. For example, if I needed to help resolving conflict within the chapter, it was important to know all the dynamics surrounding the situation (both within the organization and outside of it) so I could find a solution.

—*Sean Olmstead, Texas State University graduate student, involved with a community outreach program and LGBTQ programs*

References

Fiedler, F. (1972). The effects of leadership training and experience: A contingency model interpretation. *Administrative Science Quarterly*, *17*(4), 453–470.

Liden, R. C., & Antonakis, J. (2009). Considering context in psychological leadership research. *Human Relations*, *62*(11), 1587–1605.

Reflection Questions

- What factors or forces from the environment affect your ability to lead?

- Think back to a time when the setting and situation changed your understanding of what was needed by the leadership of a group. What happened? What adjustments were made (or should have been made)?

- What happens when leaders do not pay attention to the context?

- What contextual factors are having an impact on an organization you care about? How do they help or hurt the organization?

Chapter 22 Analyzing the Group

Interpreting group dynamics. **Analyzing the group is about recognizing that values, rules, rituals, and internal politics play a role in every group. Emotionally intelligent leaders know how to diagnose, interpret, and address these dynamics.**

Reading the Group

Every group and organization has its own values, written and unwritten rules, ways of operating, rituals, power dynamics, and internal politics. Emotionally intelligent leaders know how to diagnose, interpret, and navigate these dynamics. Imagine being in a group. Maybe it is a group you have been a part of for a long time, a new internship where you work closely with a small team, an organization or club you have just joined, or perhaps simply a group of friends. When you are new to a group, some key questions are: How do you become an integral part of that group? How do you figure out where you fit? Even if you have been a member for a long time, you may be unfamiliar with the inner workings of the group. These situations call for the EIL capacity of analyzing the group.

Colleges and universities run orientation programs so new students can learn about life on campus. If you are new to a job, you will likely attend a job orientation or some form of onboarding. Orientation programs, in college or in a workplace, aim to educate new people on everything they need to know to get started, but rarely is this enough. If you recently joined a club or organization, you may have been introduced to a few key people and given an explanation of "how we do things here." If you did, you likely heard the official or accepted rules, regulations, policies, and procedures. We all know, however, that a lot of what happens in a group is not written down, explained, or even clearly defined. In other words, group dynamics and unwritten rules exist in every group, and being aware of these is crucial for emotionally intelligent leadership.

> Sometimes, the only thing blocking progress is an ingrained animosity between two valued members. Recognizing such a dynamic is the first step in overcoming it.
> —*David Holcomb, Yale Law School graduate student*

Analyzing the group describes the knowledge and skills that help you interpret group dynamics. This EIL capacity helps you respond effectively to the group, learn and follow the established and informal rules of the group, and know how to get along without being told what to do or how to do it. This capacity helps you learn organizational politics and values and align your actions with these values. You can identify who is important in a group and how to develop relationships so you can participate more fully. You can figure out what is happening, identify the multiple roles in a group, and respond to the group accordingly.

Peeling Away the Layers

Edgar Schein (1999) introduces an onion as a metaphor for understanding the complexities of groups and organizations. On the outside are the protective layers of skin. They represent the obvious, tangible aspects of groups: who is in charge by title or position, the written rules of the group, and so on. These are the outer layers of the onion; they are easy to get at and clearly known to everyone (Hunt, 1991).

However, there are many layers, and getting involved and spending time in the organization or group exposes the different layers of organizational life. Who is actually in charge and influences the group? We have all been part of a group where the person with the title is not the most influential person in the group. What are the values of the group that drive decisions? Who forms the in-group, and who are the outsiders? When you ask these questions and discover the answers, you are analyzing the group, which helps you become more informed in your actions and decisions.

It is hard to get to the core of an onion, just like it is hard to understand the inner workings of a group. With time, purposeful analysis, and observation, you "peel back the layers" of the group and better understand what is really going on within the group. This takes both skill and intentional effort.

Digging in Deep

> Understanding a group's politics is critical, as a leader must know what avenues to utilize and which to avoid in working with others to get tasks accomplished.
>
> —*Joseph Ginley, John Carroll University sophomore, involved in the campus newspaper and campus radio station*

Diagnosing an organization or group culture is an essential skill of analyzing the group. This means identifying and understanding the many attributes of a group, which may be directly observable or beneath the surface. Verbal and nonverbal communication are directly observable attributes, while group norms and patterns of interdependence are indirectly observable attributes (Cragan & Wright, 1999). Reading the mood and energy of the group reflects your ability to diagnose a powerful yet indirectly observable attribute of a group or organization.

Identifying the key elements of organizational or group culture enhances your ability to diagnose what is happening in a group. According to Driskill and Brenton (2005), a group's culture is comprised of the following elements:

- *Symbolic elements*: Aspects of culture represent something of value, for example, logos, formal speeches, Web pages, organizational stories, mission statements, Facebook pages, even jargon used by group members.

- *Role elements*: Various roles are played in organizations, but two of the most important ones to understand are heroes (members whom everyone admires) and villains (members who are difficult or rebellious).
- *Interactive elements*: Rituals, group norms, accepted behaviors, and communication styles are demonstrated by group members and the group as a whole.
- *Context elements*: The important roles that place and time play reflect how the organization or group is affected by its history, location, and space.

Understanding these different elements enables you to interpret what is happening (and why) so that you can draw conclusions, or at least create hypotheses, to gain better insight into group dynamics. For instance, what are some symbolic elements of a popular athletic team or well-known student organization on your campus? Who are the legends and heroes on your campus? How has the team or organization shaped campus traditions over the years? How has campus location affected the growth and development of the team or organization? Becoming attuned to and navigating these elements also enhances your ability to be an active and constructive member of the group or organization.

> Usually the values of a group reflect the values of participants. If a leader cannot understand or relate to those values, let alone respect them, effective leadership can't exist.
> —*Maring Eberlein, Goucher College junior, involved in campus programming board, the equestrian team, and as a tour guide*

The Power of Asking Questions

Many of the skills that support your ability to analyze the group develop over time and develop with experience. You learn how to navigate a group by being involved and active. You develop your capacity to perceive and read social dynamics and networks of influence by becoming part of the networks themselves. Heifetz, Grashow, and Linsky (2009) describe the strategy of "being on the balcony" as one of the hallmarks of effective leadership. For instance, if you are on the balcony at a dance, you gain perspective and understanding of what is going on more easily than if you were on the dance floor itself. You can see the bigger picture by being on the balcony. With group dynamics, this means you see patterns of behavior—who is opting out of the activity, who holds the power, who is building coalitions, and so forth.

The challenge with leadership, however, is that we have to do more than just observe. We also have to be *part of the process*. Cultural anthropologists refer to this as being a participant observer. This ability to be on the balcony challenges us to act and reflect at the same time, to "stay diagnostic even as you take action" (Heifetz et al., 2009, p. 126). Obviously, this is quite difficult.

Here is an activity to try: Focus on an organization or group that you know well. It could be a club or organization, a workplace, or even a group of friends. Think about the different elements of organizational/group culture mentioned earlier. Consider these questions to get you started:

- Who is the leader of the group? What happens when that person speaks?
- What do you see as the leader's strengths and weaknesses?
- What would make the leader more successful or influential?
- What knowledge, skills, or abilities does the leader demonstrate? Did this person simply *do* a lot? Talk the most? Listen carefully?
- Who are the group members in the meeting? How are they behaving? Are they supportive or argumentative? Passive or active?
- Are group members subservient or independent-minded?
- Does anyone seem to have a personal agenda? How can you tell? How does this person interact with the leader?
- Who speaks the most, and how is this person heard? Who speaks but is not heard? How do people react to one another?

As you reflect on these questions, consider the relationship between these elements and leadership. How do these insights influence your role and your behavior in the group? Based on this information, how might you behave to move the group forward? Do you need to include and empower members? Do you need to work more effectively with a certain faction of group members? Or do you need to challenge group behaviors that are impeding the work of the group (e.g., apathy, counterproductive behavior)? Inquiry, or this process of asking many questions, plays an important role in analyzing a group and in EIL.

An Ongoing Challenge

Groups and organizations are complex and dynamic. What works in one group or for one organization may not work in another. Similarly, what works for an organization at one point in time may not work for that same organization at a different point in time. The same holds true for leadership. What works in the corporate world may not in an educational institution or on an athletic team. What influences friends may not influence team members. Analyzing the group is a capacity that improves our ability to navigate the challenges and complexities of groups and organizations.

Student Voices

Values set the standard for effective leadership. By following a set of established values, your organization will not only build upon its own reputation, but it will also create a sense of community that will enhance leadership through association.

—*Zachary Vaninger, Lewis University sophomore, involved in advisory board for the College of Business, campus board of trustees, orientation, and residence life*

Organizations divide workloads differently. I think it's important to remember that the leaders who make the largest impact are servant leaders. Understanding that serving others will make them more likely to follow your example will help an organization to grow.

—*Alexandria Whittler, Loyola University Chicago sophomore, involved in the Black cultural center*

The values of an organization are essentially the heart of an organization. Those values influence leadership because one must accept those values and live those values daily. Having an understanding of the internal dynamics of an organization helps a leader foster an environment of improvement and growth for an organization and its members.

—*Jason Castillo Sanchez, The Catholic University of America senior, involved in a Filipino cultural organization, Hispanic engineering organization, and the chemistry club*

References

Cragan, J. F., & Wright, D. W. (1999). *Communication in small groups: Theory, process, skills*. Belmont, CA: Wadsworth.

Driskill, G. W., & Brenton, A. L. (2005). *Organizational culture in action: A cultural analysis workbook*. Thousand Oaks, CA: Sage.

Heifetz, R. A., Grashow, A., & Linsky, M. (2009). Leadership in a (permanent) crisis. *Harvard Business Review*, 87(7/8), 62–69.

Hunt, J. G. (1991). *The leadership: A new synthesis*. Newbury Park, CA: Sage.

Schein, E. H. (1999). *The corporate culture survival guide*. San Francisco, CA: Jossey-Bass.

Reflection Questions

- How might analyzing the group enhance your ability to lead?

- Think about a time when you were part of a group and discovered the unwritten rules for that group. What were these rules, and how did they affect the group and its members? How did they affect you?

- How can you develop your awareness of the elements of organizational culture (symbolic, role, interactive, and context)?

- What does it look like when a leader lacks the ability to accurately analyze the group?

- Reflecting on past experience, where could the concept of "getting on the balcony" helped you lead more effectively?

Chapter 23 Assessing the Environment

Interpreting external forces and trends. **Assessing the environment is about recognizing the social, cultural, economic, and political forces that influence leadership. Emotionally intelligent leaders use their awareness of the external environment to lead effectively.**

Interpretation Is Key

> Systems thinking is a discipline for seeing wholes. It is a framework for seeing interrelationships rather than things, for seeing patterns of change rather than static "snapshots."
> —*Peter Senge, author of the book* The Fifth Discipline

Leadership does not exist in a vacuum. External factors affect an organization, its members, and those practicing leadership. Recognizing these different forces and adapting your approach to best address these is crucial for your success. One of the most difficult aspects of assessing the environment is thinking intentionally about the proverbial big picture. In many ways, we consider this happening when you are aware of, and even anticipate, the setting and situation in which you find yourself.

Being attuned to larger environmental factors affecting an organization, group, or workplace is coined within the leadership literature as systems thinking or having a systems perspective, that is, taking into account the larger environment in which the organization exists (Heifetz, 1994; Wheatley, 2005). The concept of environmental scanning, a commonly used process in the business world, addresses systems thinking through the continual monitoring and scanning of both internal and external dynamics to identify patterns, trends, threats, and opportunities

(Yukl, 2010). Through this, organizational members and leaders can alter their current and future plans accordingly. EIL encompasses an ability to engage in systems thinking and assess the environment in which we lead.

Ecology as a Metaphor

Many leadership scholars discuss the importance of the larger environment through an ecology metaphor (Heifetz, 1994; Western, 2008). Ecology focuses on the interrelations of living systems. Although an organization is not a living being in a biological sense, it is similar in that it seeks to survive, and external factors can affect its ability to do so. Imagine a tree that was recently planted. Its ability to survive and grow is based on a number of external factors such as water, sunlight, soil, and care. The tree is susceptible to external forces that may have been unexpected (e.g., a natural disaster such as a tornado) or a construction project that requires removing or replanting the tree.

> All organizations are impacted by external forces, whether it be social, political, economic, or cultural. You must realize these forces are part of a vast web of interconnectivity—what is important is finding where your organization fits in that web.
>
> —*Dylan Leigh, Fort Lewis College senior, involved in Engineers Without Borders and student government*

Now, imagine this tree is an organization. Similar external factors can affect its ability to survive. These forces may include economic, political, environmental, social, legal trends and fads; funding or financial realities; external support or challenge; and collaborations or partnerships. In general, when environmental conditions significantly change, an organism (either the tree or the organization) will either die or adapt if it is going to survive.

Organizations of all types face a number of external forces that affect their ability to thrive. Assessing the environment means we are aware of these forces (e.g., positive and negative, opportunities and threats), determine the influence of these forces, and lead the organization accordingly. On campus, for instance, assessing the environment includes:

- knowing campus policies and procedures;
- creating and managing relationships with other organizations on campus and in the community;
- identifying sources of funding and support from the institution;
- assessing how societal, campus, and student trends may influence the relevancy of the organization;
- working with influential stakeholders outside of the organization, such as alumni; and
- understanding the community.

> External forces have led to constant changes and the persistent need for adaptation within my organization.
> —*Khaliq Martin, York University sophomore, involved in the Caribbean students association*

Take, for example, an interest-based student organization on campus, such as the College Republicans or the Accounting Club. Assessing the environment means knowing campus regulations and factors that could affect the organization, such as recognition processes, organizational policies, and other organizations and events on campus. Expanding the scope further, being aware of factors outside the campus community, such as political trends or recent election results could affect the College Republicans' events. Likewise, new laws could alter the content of professional development trainings hosted by the Accounting Club. If one of these organizations fails to be attuned to these external factors, the organization may not remain relevant and could suffer. Assessing the environment helps you identify opportunities to enhance the organization such as an event in the community, a relevant documentary, or a similar organization at a nearby campus with which you can collaborate.

Scanning the Environment

To get a sense of how to recognize the influence of the environment on leadership, try an experiment. The next time you attend a meeting at work or an event of an organization in which you are involved, pay close attention to what is going on around you. Think about the experience as a whole. As mentioned in the previous chapter, remember the importance of inquiry and *getting on the balcony*. Observe the following environmental factors and how they affect what is happening:

- Are its activities and mission (reason for existence) consistent with the campus community? The larger community?
- Are members and leaders in sync with the interests and needs of the student body? The campus community?
- Is there pride in the organization? Is it doing well in the eyes of its members? Of its organizational partners, allies, or supporters?
- Is the campus community supportive of the organization?
- Is the organization seen as a benefit or detriment to the community?

As you reflect on these questions (and others), imagine yourself as an external consultant or anthropologist trying to observe the organization and these dynamics from the outside. Notice but do not engage. What conclusions can you draw about the organization through this perspective? How can you use these conclusions to inform your actions? Assessing the environment means you observe and diagnose so that when you take action, you are more informed. Taking this to the next level, the real challenge lies in being able to observe the organization from a broader perspective while also engaging within the organization. Leadership scholar Donald Schön (1984) calls this "reflection in action," which is similar to getting on the balcony, as discussed in the previous chapter (Heifetz, 1994).

This difficult, yet crucial, skill for emotionally intelligent leadership must be practiced intentionally. Why? For most of us, it is easiest to jump in and react to stimuli or default to preprogrammed responses rather than observe. It is also easy to lose sight of the big picture and focus on only what is in front of you. Learning how and what to observe comes with experience and deliberate practice. What can you do to boost your capacity to assess the environment? Try to notice how the larger community affects an organization's events or leaders' decisions. Leaders who are aware of their environment use that knowledge of key external forces to determine a course of action. Where do you see this happening?

Embracing Uncertainty

> I try to adapt my plans accordingly to prepare for unexpected circumstances. There's always going to be a situation that changes the game, and I prepare myself to be open and willing to modify my plans.
> —*Jenna Kreitman, University of Michigan junior, involved in Greek life*

Although a key aim of assessing the environment is to be aware of and prepare for changes in the external environment, there are aspects of the environment that we cannot anticipate or control. Margaret Wheatley (2005), a prominent leadership scholar, suggests, "No matter how hard we work to create a stable and healthy organization, our organization will continue to experience dramatic changes far beyond our control" (p. 146). Because uncertainty is inevitable, it is important that we learn to embrace this uncertainty and work with it rather than resist or fight it. Phillip Clampitt and Robert DeKoch (2001), authors of *Embracing Uncertainty: The Essence of Leadership*, write, "The chaos, complexity, and speed of change in modern organizations require that effective leaders become masters of embracing uncertainty" (p. 6). Embracing uncertainty allows us to be more open and flexible to changing situations. When we do this, we also discover new opportunities and find creative solutions and innovation.

Student Voices

Some forces I have seen that affect organizations are family life drama, monetary concerns, and intergroup conflict.

—*Carolyn Kriebel, John Carroll University junior, involved in a leadership program and a community religious organization*

The fact is, things will happen that will affect your organization, no matter how much time and energy you spend on preparing for the unexpected. All you can do is keep a positive attitude, learn from the experience, and keep moving forward.

—*Jonathan Martinez, Texas A&M University junior, involved in an extended orientation program, traditions council, and leadership organizations*

As a leader, I first take a step back to observe the situation and listen. Listening allows a leader to accurately judge the best course of action.

—*Cole Lawson, University of Missouri sophomore, involved in dance marathon, alternative winter break, leadership organizations, a community music program, a peer mentoring program, and as a teaching assistant for a leadership class*

References

Clampitt, P. G., & DeKoch, R. J. (2001). *Embracing uncertainty: The essence of leadership*. Armonk, NY: M.E. Sharpe.

Heifetz, R. A. (1994). *Leadership without easy answers*. Cambridge, MA: Harvard University Press.

Schön, D. A. (1984). *The reflective practitioner: How professionals think in action.* New York, NY: Better Books.

Western, S. (2008). *Leadership: A critical text.* London, England: Sage.

Wheatley, M. J. (2005). *Finding our way: Leadership for an uncertain time.* San Francisco, CA: Berrett-Koehler.

Yukl, G. (2010). *Leadership in organizations* (7th ed.). Upper Saddle River, NJ: Prentice Hall.

Reflection Questions

- What external forces have affected organizations in which you have been involved?

- What external forces can you anticipate affecting your organization or workplace in the future?

- If you're involved in a student organization, what school or campus dynamics do you see as providing opportunities or threats to your organization's future?

- When have you engaged in reflection-in-action? How does this compare to simply acting?

- How can you better embrace uncertainty in your life? In your organization?

Chapter 24 Developing Emotionally Intelligent Leadership

A natural ending for a book on leadership is to provide some suggestions for practice. After all, we hope that you are now wondering what this all means for you. What are the next steps? In other words, how do you develop emotionally intelligent leadership (EIL)?

A foundational concept of EIL is consciousness of self, which is why we started the book with this facet. How, you may be asking, do you increase your self-awareness? To put it succinctly, prepare yourself—because it takes a lot of hard work, and it is truly a lifelong activity. Although we could create a long list of ingredients for development, here are two that we suggest as good places to begin:

1. *Get to know YOU*. Be known as someone who seeks out, and is open to, feedback. Exist in a continuous state of reflection.
2. *Seek out challenge and support*. Associate with people who challenge and support you. Seek out environments that will help you grow and that help you become your best self.

Get to Know *You*

In many ways we are ending where we began. Developing self-awareness is an intentional process, like the development of any other knowledge, skill, or ability. As we've suggested, an important way to learn more about yourself, and thereby increase your self-awareness, is to seek feedback from those who know you best. To do this, ask yourself whether you respond well to feedback. If the answer to this question is "Maybe" or

"No," then you know you have more work to do. Have courage and faith—the more you seek out feedback, the more you learn and the easier it gets. Try to become known as a person who is willing to accept and act upon the suggestions made by peers, mentors, and family (when it's appropriate). Before you know it, you may receive feedback without asking for it—and, more often than not, this is a good indication that you are demonstrating an active commitment to self-knowledge.

Along with openness to feedback, reflection is a crucial component of development. Reflection takes many forms. For some, it is through writing, blogging, or keeping a journal. For others, it happens through conversations with others. Some may reflect while they exercise or drive in their cars. Regardless of how you reflect, make sure you *do* reflect. One of the worst mistakes to make in a leadership role is to focus solely on doing more and staying active. Skipping reflection minimizes your ability to recognize your mistakes, identify important connections, and integrate your experiences with your ideas.

After all, it is in reflection that learning occurs. Think about it—football players watch tapes of their games and musicians listen to their recorded performances. These are all forms of reflection. Focus on how consciousness of self, consciousness of others, and consciousness of context play into your experience. Most important, take the necessary time to look at yourself in the mirror. As humans, we tend to externalize. In other words, we blame others when we fail. When you take time to reflect, be sure to examine what you did well and what you did not do well. This helps you celebrate your successes and learn from your mistakes.

Seek Out Challenge *and* Support

Surround yourself with people who want to support your growth and development. Let friends, family members, mentors, coaches, and co-workers know you want to improve and develop. By doing so, you will invite them to help you, and they can help hold you accountable to the goals you have identified. Sharing with others that you want to improve yourself can be challenging because it places you in a vulnerable position. However, when others know you are trying to learn something new, they tend to be more understanding of mistakes and perhaps more interested in helping you learn.

Another essential aspect of your development is your environment. Place yourself in situations and settings that offer appropriate levels of challenge and support (McCauley & Van Velsor, 2003; Sanford, 1967). Are the people in your environment helpful and, at the same time, able to challenge you? Are there people who are barriers to your overall development because they are either too supportive or too hard on you? Are there forces in the environment that overwhelm you because of their complexity? Or is the environment so lenient that you can do whatever you want and it doesn't matter? Your environment is one of the most important and overlooked aspects of development. When you surround yourself with people who embody who you hope to become, you will have a better chance of becoming that person. When your environment pushes you and supports you in your growth, you are more likely to develop your capacity for leadership.

Likewise, we suggest placing yourself in environments where you can deliberately practice the capacities you hope to develop. We call these *edge experiences*. You know you are at your edge when you have a nervous feeling in your stomach—a feeling of uncertainty as to how things will turn out. For some, this may be managing conflict; for others, it may be inspiring others or taking on a formal leadership role. Being at the edge requires some risk taking, and it is through this risk taking that there is often much reward and learning. What is your edge? What experiences will take your abilities to a new level? Who can help you along the way? Clarity around these questions is paramount as you strive to develop your leadership capacities.

Conclusion

Along with these specific suggestions, we share a multitude of ideas for development in the *Emotionally Intelligent Leadership for Students: Student Workbook* and the *Emotionally Intelligent Leadership for Students: Inventory*. Each of these resources provides opportunities to explore the three facets and nineteen capacities of EIL at a deeper level. Likewise, there are retreats, workshops, courses, certificates, and degrees on campus and in your community. Take advantage of these opportunities and build a strong and caring network of peers.

Finally, remember that you will never be finished with this work. The process of development will keep you in a continual state of investigation. What works in one situation may not work in another. What was successful last week may not be successful next week. What worked for you in the classroom may not work for you on your team. So how do you know when to adjust your course? Often, you know you need to alter your strategies when things are too easy or too difficult. This means that if everything comes too easily, you're likely in a situation that is so comfortable that you're missing out on opportunities to grow and develop. Conversely, if you keep meeting challenge after challenge, never quite feeling that you're succeeding, then it is likely that your environment is too challenging. In these cases, you may find the capacities you are currently demonstrating are not enough, or not well suited to get you where you hope to be. In either case, you may want to think about how to adjust course or develop a capacity that does not come naturally to improve your situation.

In the end, all of us have an opportunity to engage in leadership. Some of us will monitor this process intentionally and some will not. This book is a guide to help you identify the critical capacities necessary for becoming more effective. EIL is about combining your natural abilities with greater awareness and hard work. You have your own unique set of talents and capacities. And you have the potential to develop more. We wish you the best on your path and hope you are successful in making your dreams, and the dreams of others, a reality.

References

McCauley, C. D., & Van Velsor, E. (Eds.). (2003). *The Center for Creative Leadership handbook of leadership development.* San Francisco, CA: Jossey-Bass.

Sanford, N. (1967). *Self and society: Social change and individual development.* New York, NY: Atherton Press.

Appendix EIL Overview

Emotionally intelligent leadership (EIL) promotes an intentional focus on three facets: consciousness of self, consciousness of others, and consciousness of context. Across the three EIL facets are nineteen capacities that equip individuals with the knowledge, skills, perspectives, and attitudes to achieve desired leadership outcomes.

Consciousness of Self

Demonstrating emotionally intelligent leadership involves awareness of your abilities, emotions, and perceptions. Consciousness of self is about prioritizing the inner work of reflection and introspection and appreciating that self-awareness is a continual and ongoing process.

- *Emotional Self-Perception*: Identifying emotions and their influence on behavior. Emotional self-perception is about describing, naming, and understanding your emotions. Emotionally intelligent leaders are aware of how situations influence emotions and how emotions affect interactions with others.
- *Emotional Self-Control*: Consciously moderating emotions. Emotional self-control means intentionally managing your emotions and understanding how and when to demonstrate them appropriately. Emotionally intelligent leaders take responsibility for regulating their emotions and are not victims of them.
- *Authenticity*: Being transparent and trustworthy. Authenticity is about developing credibility, being transparent, and aligning

words with actions. Emotionally intelligent leaders live their values and present themselves and their motives in an open and honest manner.

- *Healthy Self-Esteem*: Having a balanced sense of self. Healthy self-esteem is about balancing confidence in your abilities with humility. Emotionally intelligent leaders are resilient and remain confident when faced with setbacks and challenges.
- *Flexibility*: Being open and adaptive to change. Flexibility is about adapting your approach and style based on changing circumstances. Emotionally intelligent leaders seek input and feedback from others and adjust accordingly.
- *Optimism*: Having a positive outlook. Optimism is about setting a positive tone for the future. Emotionally intelligent leaders use optimism to foster hope and generate energy.
- *Initiative*: Taking action. Initiative means being a self-starter and being motivated to take the first step. Emotionally intelligent leaders are ready to take action, demonstrate interest, and capitalize on opportunities.
- *Achievement*: Striving for excellence. Achievement is about setting high personal standards and getting results. Emotionally intelligent leaders strive to improve and are motivated by an internal drive to succeed.

Consciousness of Others

Demonstrating emotionally intelligent leadership involves awareness of the abilities, emotions, and perceptions of others. Consciousness of others is about intentionally working with and influencing individuals and groups to bring about positive change.

- *Displaying Empathy*: Being emotionally in tune with others. Empathy is about perceiving and addressing the emotions of others. Emotionally intelligent leaders place a high value on the feelings of others and respond to their emotional cues.
- *Inspiring Others*: Energizing individuals and groups. Inspiration occurs when people are excited about a better future.

Emotionally intelligent leaders foster feelings of enthusiasm and commitment to organizational mission, vision, and goals.

- *Coaching Others*: Enhancing the skills and abilities of others. Coaching is about helping others enhance their skills, talents, and abilities. Emotionally intelligent leaders know they cannot do everything themselves and create opportunities for others to develop.
- *Capitalizing on Difference*: Benefiting from multiple perspectives. Capitalizing on difference means recognizing that our unique identities, perspectives, and experiences are assets, not barriers. Emotionally intelligent leaders appreciate and use difference as an opportunity to create a broader perspective.
- *Developing Relationships*: Building a network of trusting relationships. Developing relationships means creating meaningful connections. Emotionally intelligent leaders encourage opportunities for relationships to grow and develop.
- *Building Teams*: Working with others to accomplish a shared purpose. Building teams is about effectively communicating, creating a shared purpose, and clarifying roles to get results. Emotionally intelligent leaders foster group cohesion and develop a sense of "we."
- *Demonstrating Citizenship*: Fulfilling responsibilities to the group. Citizenship is about being actively engaged and following through on your commitments. Emotionally intelligent leaders meet their ethical and moral obligations for the benefit of others and the larger purpose.
- *Managing Conflict*: Identifying and resolving conflict. Managing conflict is about working through differences to facilitate the group process. Emotionally intelligent leaders skillfully and confidently address conflicts to find the best solution.
- *Facilitating Change*: Working toward new directions. Facilitating change is about advancing ideas and initiatives through innovation and creativity. Emotionally intelligent leaders seek to improve on the status quo and mobilize others toward a better future.

Consciousness of Context

Demonstrating emotionally intelligent leadership involves awareness of the setting and situation. Consciousness of context is about paying attention to how environmental factors and internal group dynamics affect the process of leadership.

- *Analyzing the Group*: Interpreting group dynamics. Analyzing the group is about recognizing that values, rules, rituals, and internal politics play a role in every group. Emotionally intelligent leaders know how to diagnose, interpret, and address these dynamics.
- *Assessing the Environment*: Interpreting external forces and trends. Assessing the environment is about recognizing the social, cultural, economic, and political forces that influence leadership. Emotionally intelligent leaders use their awareness of the external environment to lead effectively.

INDEX

R

T

U

V

If you enjoyed this book, you may also like these:

Emotionally Intelligent Leadership for Students: Student Workbook, 2nd Edition
by Marcy Levy Shankman, Scott J. Allen, Paige Haber-Curran
ISBN: 9781118821824

Emotionally Intelligent Leadership for Students: Facilitation and Activity Guide, 2nd Edition
by Marcy Levy Shankman, Scott J. Allen, Paige Haber-Curran
ISBN: 9781118821770

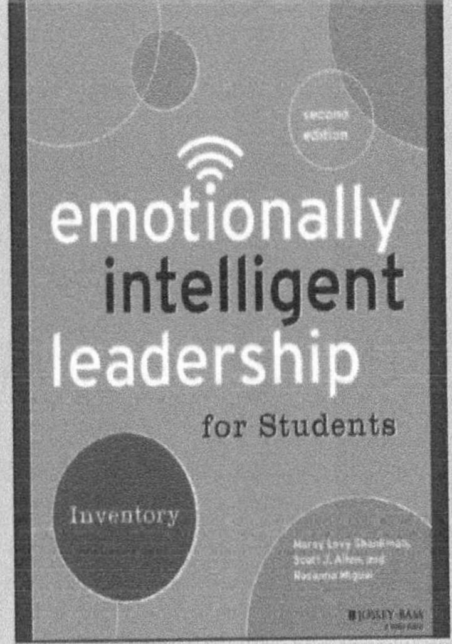

Emotionally Intelligent Leadership for Students: Inventory, 2nd Edition
by Marcy Levy Shankman, Scott J. Allen, Rosanna Miguel
ISBN: 9781118821664

Want to connect?

Like us on Facebook
https://www.facebook.com/JBHigherEd

Follow us on Twitter
https://twitter.com/JBHigherEd